ADAM AND EVE

The Spiritual Symbolism of Genesis and Exodus

S. D. Fohr

UNIVERSITY
PRESS OF
AMERICA

LANHAM • NEW YORK • LONDON

Copyright © 1986 by

University Press of America,® Inc.

4720 Boston Way
Lanham, MD 20706

3 Henrietta Street
London WC2E 8LU England

Library of Congress Cataloging in Publication Data

Fohr, S. D., 1943-
 Adam and Eve : the spiritual symbolism of Genesis
and Exodus.

 Bibliography: p.
 Includes index.
 1. Bible. O.T. Genesis—Criticism, interpretation,
etc.   2. Bible. O.T. Exodus—Criticism, interpretation,
etc.   3. Symbolism in the Bible.   I. Title.
BS1235.2.F58   1986   222'.11064   86-1497
ISBN 0-8191-5267-6 (alk. paper)
ISBN 0-8191-5268-4 (pbk. : alk. paper)

All University Press of America books are produced on acid-free
paper which exceeds the minimum standards set by the National
Historical Publications and Records Commission.

To Rena, who helps to complete me.

Acknowledgments

I would like to thank the following publishers for permission to quote copyrighted material: The Jewish Publication Society for passages from The Torah Copyright ©1962 and The Prophets Copyright ©1978 by The Jewish Publication Society, The University of Chicago Press for passages from Moses Maimonides' The Guide of the Perplexed translated by Shlomo Pines ©1963 by the University of Chicago, and Paulist Press and The Society for Promoting Christian Knowledge for passages from Gregory of Nyssa: The Life of Moses translated by Abraham J. Malherbe and Everett Ferguson Copyright ©1978 by The Missionary Society of St. Paul the Apostle in the State of New York.

I am indebted to Professor George Mavrodes of the University of Michigan for demonstrating the unreasonableness of typical modern arguments against the existence of spiritual realities. I also owe much to Professor David N. Freedman of the University of Michigan for all that he taught me about the Bible and for his support of the publishing of this book. Further, I gratefully acknowledge the help I have received from Swami Bhashyananda, Head of the Vivekananda-Vedanta Society of Chicago, in learning about the Hindu tradition, especially Advaita Vedanta.

I must especially thank my father, Henry Fohr, for his expert translations of many difficult passages in Guénon's untranslated works. Without his help this book could not have been written.

Finally, I would like to express my gratitude to Lynne Chiles who typed all drafts of the manuscript, put up with the many little changes that were made in it, and provided many excellent suggestions for improving it.

All translations of verses in Genesis and Exodus are from The Torah, published in Philadelphia by the Jewish Publication Society, Second Edition, 1967. This translation is based on the oldest complete Hebrew version, the Masoretic Text.

All translations of verses in Isaiah and Ezekiel are from The Prophets, also published by the Jewish Publication Society, 1978.

All translations of verses in the New Testament are from The New English Bible, published in England by the Oxford and Cambridge University Presses, Second Edition, 1970.

Analytic Table of Contents

Preface

The symbolism of the Bible has been expounded from at least 200 B.C. by Jewish writers and by both Jewish and Christian writers throughout the Christian Era. In addition, there has been no lack of Islamic commentators on those parts of the Old Testament which have been incorporated into the Qur'an. We might mention in particular Philo, Origen and St. Gregory of Nyssa in ancient times, Maimonides, Al-Ghazzali and Al-Arabi in the middle ages, and René Guénon in our own century. Unfortunately, in spite of all the symbolic interpretations of scripture which have been available for over 2000 years, most believers are unaware of this dimension of the text they consider sacred. Those studies of Biblical symbolism which have been done by the aforementioned authors and others have two characteristics. First, they are geared more for the specialist (or the elect) than the layman. Second, with the exception of Philo, they treat the symbolism of the Bible on a piecemeal basis. This second point is not meant as a criticism. The aim of a writer like Guénon was to examine certain symbols wherever they occurred in religions and other spiritual traditions throughout the world. If such symbols occurred in the Bible then they were explained in that context. While the others were not concerned with explaining the symbolism of traditions other than their own, with the one exception noted, they picked their subjects carefully rather than aim at comprehensiveness. It is our goal to bring the symbolic dimension of Genesis and Exodus to the attention of the typical believer, and to do so in a systematic manner which is accessible and rewarding to the specialist and layman alike.

The ending of the book may seem a little abrupt to some readers, but it is meant to produce a certain effect. It is an aim of our book to be spiritually rewarding as well as informative. This applies to the footnotes as well as the body of the book, and we urge readers to give them due consideration.

.

Chapter 1 - Introduction

a. The Esoteric and the Exoteric

Whatever the terms "esoteric" and "exoteric" may designate in the thinking of some people, it is clear that first and foremost they refer to the two main ways of approaching God that are open to human beings. As the etymologies of these words indicate, one way is internal and the other external. That is to say, one may strive for the inner realization of one's essential identity with God, or one may take up the devotional attitude of a loving servant doing the master's bidding.[1] Implicit in the second attitude is the idea that God is totally external and other, while the first involves the idea that really knowing ourselves is tantamount to knowing God. Both attitudes can be present in a person, and from the standpoint of our individuality we must never cease to view ourselves as servants. But the esoteric approach involves an attempt to see ourselves from another standpoint in which our relationship to God will be viewed accordingly.

It has been said, not without good reason, that religion is an essentially exoteric phenomenon. For if we consider the three major religions, Judaism, Christianity, and Islam, it is obvious that for many centuries they have stressed the devotional approach. However, besides the presence of esoteric groups within the sphere of influence of these religions, we must also point to the esoteric character of many of the writings which are recognized by them as canonical. Some of the most striking passages occur in the Gospel of John[2] and those interpreters with an especially exoteric bent have a great deal of trouble explaining these passages and rather try to avoid them altogether. Yet such ideas are like the supporting columns of a building which cannot be removed without the whole edifice crumbling.[3]

The generally exoteric nature of religions is shown by the stress placed on worshiping, God publicly and following God's commandments. Indeed, the typical believer of today thinks that living a good life (as defined by scripture and/or religious authorities) and attending services at synagogue, church or mosque are the keys to salvation. It is to be noted that both of these practices have to do with the outer life of the believer, i.e., with what is external to him. And we may add that the God he is supposed to love and worship

1

as well as the Heaven he is supposed to reach are also taken to be external to the believer.

Perhaps the clearest way of distinguishing the exoteric from the esoteric approach to God is to examine what each has to say about the subject of holy war. From the exoteric viewpoint, which has been that of organized religion, a holy war is something completely external in which "heathens" are converted, or put to death, or at least put to flight. From the esoteric viewpoint a holy war is something that goes on within a human being and involves a sort of inner conversion and death. In fact, the waging of the inner war constitutes the whole of esoteric practice.[4]

In the esoteric approach the emphasis is not so much on outer activity as on inner activity with the goal of gaining knowledge of one's innermost being, for God is understood as the center point or heart of the believer. Basically this approach involves two initiatic deaths and rebirths which have as their goals the perfection of the human state and the "escape" from its limitations.[5] Thus the journey to Heaven is an inner one which does not have to wait on bodily death. In fact, immortality is understood in a completely different way in exotericism and esotericism. One of the problems with the exoteric approach is that it tends to understand everything in crude spatio-temporal terms. Thus salvation is understood as living forever in a place called Heaven. On the other hand, salvation from the esoteric approach, which is more properly called liberation or deliverance, involves penultimately a residing in consciousness at the still center point of one's being (the point of the "actionless activity" of God), and ultimately an awareness of one's essential identity with God. In either case one achieves a sense of eternity (or timelessness), which is the esoteric understanding of "immortality."

At once it will be objected that we have misunderstood those who engage in the typical religious or exoteric approach to God, for they too are concerned with the inner life, seeking inspiration through prayer. We can readily admit that this is true to some degree, but we must also say that many who think they have found inspiration are deluded. We are referring to the practitioners of what can be called emotionalistic religion, for they have mistaken heightened emotional states for inspiration. It may well be that certain very inspired people down through the centuries often experienced heightened emotional states, but we should not confuse or equate these states with inspiration. Besides, even real inspiration should not be confused with realization which is the true goal of the esoteric approach.

It will also be objected that those who take the esoteric approach are merely being self-centered. This is a simplistic view which does not hold up under close scrutiny. There is little doubt that many who think they are on the esoteric path are laboring under delusions, and this whether they have been initiated or not. But there are those who are truly preparing themselves for a time when they can be of inestimable value to the rest of the world. We must keep in mind the phrase "physician heal thyself." It is impossible to be a "force for good" in the world if one is filled with egoism and overwhelming desires, and the negative emotions they engender. All the "shalt nots" in the world cannot remove the inner turmoil that causes outer strife. While exotericism deals almost entirely with the outer man, esotericism addresses itself directly to the inner $_6$man and is able, indirectly, to effect the outer man.^{6}

Before going any further in contrasting the esoteric and exoteric approaches to God it is necessary, in order to avoid misunderstandings, to point out that mysticism is an exoteric or essentially religious development. Unfortunately, the term "mystic" has changed meanings over the centuries and this has led to a great deal of confusion. The mystic who took part in the ancient mysteries was definitely engaged in an esoteric venture, but for the most part, those called mystics in the Judaeo-Christian tradition have been squarely within the province of exotericism. There have been exceptions to this, but we are concerned with the general rule. A practitioner of the esoteric way takes an active posture with respect to his spiritual development. There are definite practices which are guided by a spiritual master. The typical mystic adopts a rather passive attitude, praying and hoping for Divine inspiration and often being subject to various visions. Then too, the mystic views himself as separate from God, although he seeks to be united to Him. The mystic is the artist of the soul, and is inspired much in the way a poet, painter or composer is inspired. Only his inspiration takes his life as its canvas.

3

b. Unity and Division

The word "believer" for a practitioner of religion is quite suggestive, and contrasts sharply with "knower" which is an apt description of one who has made progress on the esoteric path. And it is not a matter of the latter knowing what the former only believes, for the subject matter is different in the two cases. In the case of the believer we are in the realm of dogma whereas in the case of the latter we are in the realm of that sort of knowledge where knower and known are one. There is no doubt that belief is of central importance for those on the exoteric path, since the holding of certain beliefs is considered necessary for salvation in all of the major faiths. Now there are certain beliefs that are surely very central from the religious perspective, e.g., that the universe is a creation of God, that (in this context) the believer is a creature, and that God is perfectly good. But there are other beliefs that are insisted upon in many of the religious sects that are not at all central, e.g., that the universe is approximately 6000 years old, that it was given its form in six days, and that the story of Adam and Eve is an historical account.[7] In addition to these, there are particular doctrinal matters having to do with key concepts and practices which are also stressed. The end result is a sort of recipe theory of salvation according to which if you believe such and such and do so and so you are saved. Not surprisingly, the different religions, as well as sects within the religions, put forward different recipes,[8] a matter which, though not serious in itself, can lead to serious consequences.

As members of these different groups tend to identify themselves by adherence to the full set of their beliefs (their complete dogma), religions and sects tend to divide people. This is exacerbated by what we might call the meta-religious belief according to which the believer's particular salvation recipe is the only one which will work.[9] All of this results in a we-they dichotomy where the "we" are taken as saved and the "they" as damned. And on the principle that "he who isn't with us is against us," hostility is developed toward other groups, a hostility that results in one of two outcomes. The "we" may try to convert the "they" by reasoning or by force, or the "we" may decide that the "they" are somehow less than human and can be slaughtered like animals.[10] The exoteric approach carries the idea of winners and losers into the sphere of salvation. It is as if salvation is the prize of a special kind of Olympic games entered by

4

various religions. Since there can be only one overall winner it means that many whole groups must be losers. Those who judge "Whoever is for the Lord" (Exodus, Chapter 32, Verse 26) by the acceptance of their particular set of beliefs have something less than love in their hearts.

On the other hand, the esoteric approach tends to unite people, for the tenets of esotericism are shared by all of the major religions as well as all other true spiritual traditions.[11] Different groups are not seen as enemies but as seeking God in their own way.[12] There is no question here of watering down spirituality to its lowest common denominator (which is being done, in quite a different way, in our own time). The esoteric side of religions is their most profound and spiritual part.

There is a commonly held exoteric view that all of the various spiritual traditions of the world are not up to the same thing in that they do not all promote the same high ethical standards. In particular, the received view is that the spiritual traditions of the East do not involve the high standards of the religions of the West.[13] If true, this would certainly be damning, for the outwardly moral life is a preliminary for any spiritual advancement as well as an indication of such advancement. But the bloody history of the West during the last 3000 years belies any kind of chauvinistic comparison with the East. Probably the only antidote to this sort of poisonous view is an extended visit to the East coupled with an objective look at the treatment people accord each other in the West. The social teachings of the East, which are the equivalent of ethics minus the latter's emotive content, are for all intents and purposes the same as those of the West.[14]

c. Literal and Symbolic

[15]Adapting Friedrich von Hügel's masterful analysis[15] we may say that all people first become acquainted with religions through their exoteric dimension. It cannot be otherwise since, as we have already said, religion is basically exoteric in character. A majority of people never go beyond this first stage, which we will call the childish stage of belief. It is childish because we are urged to accept what we are told without question, even if what we are expected to believe is highly implausible, e.g., the

5

historical truth of all the stories in the Bible. A significant minority questions the historical truth of these stories as well as the dogmas of their religion. Some of these people, feeling that religion is a tissue of lies, never go beyond this stage and become atheists, or at best agnostics. Or perhaps they do not have quite so strong a reaction and grudgingly accept Bible stories as fictional tales whose purpose is to teach certain lessons. People in this latter group live out their lives in a state of lukewarm faith bordering on atheism. But some realize that there is another dimension to religion and go beyond this second stage. They discover the esoteric writings of those connected with initiatic groups and learn of the inner life and the inner meaning of Bible stories. These people take up the life of the spirit as best they can, and we may call this third stage the mature practice of religion.[16]

In light of this analysis, what must one think of the view that questioning the historic truth of Bible stories undermines religious belief? If by "religious belief" is meant unquestioning assent to what one is told, a sort of parroting back of what one has heard with no real inner development, then we must agree that such questioning undermines religious belief, i.e., childish religious belief.[17] On the other hand, if by religious belief is meant a life chosen by oneself based on repentance and conscious spiritual striving, then questioning the historical truth of Bible stories may well be the first step toward religious belief. It is a strange irony that the literalistic view of how one should read the Bible to get the most out of it is not only not true, but is the very opposite of the truth.

But there is still more to be said in answer to this question, for there is an important matter which cannot be avoided. In a way, turning from the exoteric approach to the Bible does undermine religious belief, but not so as to produce a negative result from the spiritual perspective. It undermines the "belief" aspect of religions which, as we have said, is responsible for their particular form. Thus the mature phase involves, in a sense, a breaking out of the confines of a religion while still using it as a base. However, from a wider perspective we can reiterate that religions do contain esoteric ideas in their canonical works, and this is especially true of <u>Genesis</u> and much of <u>Exodus</u>, which are the concerns of this book. So by adopting the esoteric perspective which involves interpreting many passages symbolically, we are not really leaving the sphere of religion.

The importance of not adopting a literalistic approach to the Bible is explained very clearly by both Origen[18] and Maimonides.[19] Much of Maimonides' work, The Guide of the Perplexed, deals with the perplexities engendered by a literal reading of the Torah, and his comments center on the description of God and His actions. If we were to take the story of Adam and Eve in a crude spatio-temporal way, we would have a picture of God as a superhuman being who takes walks around the Garden of Eden. Furthermore, we would have to view Him as a vindictive being, jealous of His prerogatives, who punishes people for learning of the difference between good and evil. It is not surprising that a thoughtful person might either throw up his hands at the whole thing, or at least decide that such a God was not worthy of worship. This last reaction was indeed that of the Gnostics, as Origen mentions. They viewed the God described[20] in Genesis as an inferior being to the Most High God.

Origen and Maimonides agree that the Bible itself provides hints that certain of its material is to be interpreted symbolically. In his book, On First Principles, Origen mentions "certain stumbling blocks or interruptions of the narrative meaning" which take the form of "impossibilities and contradictions." Maimonides likens the stories of the Torah to articles of gold covered by filigree work of silver. The filigree work has small holes in it which can be seen if examined closely. These holes correspond to the indications in the stories that something deeper and of much greater value is hidden within them. We will discuss some of these indications in subsequent chapters.

Neither Maimonides nor Origen deny that the literal meaning of most of the Bible is valuable. The laws and the morals drawn from many of the stories are beneficial externally for societies and individuals alike. We can go further and say that an appreciation of the literal meaning can lead a person to the point where an appreciation of the symbolic meaning is possible, for there are always two stages in spiritual growth, one preparatory and the other active. But we must agree with both Maimonides and Origen that some of the Biblical narratives cannot be swallowed in a literal way without harmful effects. We may choose to put them aside, but that is merely avoiding the issue.

Besides providing hints about what is to be taken symbolically, the Bible explicitly refers to the use of symbolic stories for the purpose of teaching wisdom.[21] And once one has become aware that symbolic interpre-

7

tations of ancient "historical" texts are commonplace in other cultures, and that certain items which are prominent in Bible stories (e.g., the tree and the snake) were almost universally understood to symbolize specific things in ancient times, one can hardly avoid the conclusion that certain parts of Scripture, though they may strike the modern mind as historical narratives, are to be understood symbolically.

There are many people who are distrustful of symbolic interpretations except where allegories or parables are clearly identified as such (e.g., in Ezekiel and the Gospels). They usually attempt to explain away the "impossibilities and contradictions" we mentioned earlier. They believe that anyone who interprets Bible stories symbolically is "reading something into them" and perverting their intended meaning. In light of what we have already said this distrustful attitude is uncalled for. And we may add that attempts to explain away unpalatable aspects of certain Bible stories have been uniformly unsuccessful. Besides invoking hypotheses for which there is no evidence and twisting the obvious meanings of words, they smack of trying to make the best of a bad situation. Instead of all this twisting and turning it behooves us to look beneath the surface of things. If we do, we will find that everything makes sense.

d. Individual Symbols and Allegories

It has been said that to those with understanding everything in creation is a symbol. We would like to put emphasis on the phrase "to those with understanding." There are no symbols without intellects to comprehend them as such, just as there are no sounds (although there may be sound waves) without senses and souls to perceive them as such. This feature of symbols leads to a problem in expounding the symbolism of the Bible in the present age. But before we explain this more fully it will be well to make some general comments about symbols.

Put simply, symbols are things which stand for other things. That is to say, they are taken by rational beings as pointing beyond themselves. We can most easily divide symbols into two categories: natural and artificial (or conventional). Examples of the former, which are the most important ones as far as spiritual matters are concerned, are human beings, fathers, mothers, children, brothers, heaven (sky), earth, atmosphere, rain, waters, mountains, caves, hearts, snakes, the sun and its rays, the moon, the stars, trees, flowers, rocks, meteorites, fire, smoke, sexual union, wine, and drunkenness. The most obvious example of the latter are words and pictures, although anything made by man can fall into this category. For instance, the human institution of marriage, which in a way corresponds to sexual union, has functioned as a very important symbol in Kabbalism. Among the most important linguistic symbols are names, such as "Cain" (which stands in most people's minds for fratricide and evil in general) and the book title "Nineteen Eighty-Four" (which stands for an oppressive world situation).

We have been focusing on individual symbols, but alongside of them stand symbolic stories, and these too can be natural or artificial. Besides actual episodes in the lives of individual people and nations we can say that the development of our realm of existence can be seen as a symbolic story. On the artificial level there are what are usually called allegories and parables, where one group of events is meant to symbolize another group of events. It is clear in these cases that the literal meaning of the story is merely a vehicle for expressing the symbolic meaning, or to put it another way, the original story is just an oblique way of saying something else which can be said directly.

Gershom Scholem, evidently following Goethe in his conceptualizations, expresses the view that there are two sorts of non-literal interpretations of Scripture which he refers to as symbolization and allegorization:

> The thing which becomes a symbol retains its original form and its original content. It does not become, so to speak, an empty shell into which another content is poured; in itself, through its own existence, it makes another reality transparent which cannot appear in any other form. If the allegory can be defined as the representation of an expressible something by another expressible something, the mystical symbol is an expressible representation of something which lies beyond the sphere of expression and communication, something which comes from a sphere whose face is, as it were, turned inward and away from us. A hidden and inexpressible reality

9

finds its expression in the symbol
. . . .Where deeper insight into the
structure of the allegory uncovers
fresh layers of meaning, the symbol
is intuitively understood all at
once--or not at all.[22]

There is an implication in this analysis that
allegorization somehow devalues the events of a story.
On the other hand, symbolization would understand the
events and characters as paralleling something in a
higher realm, and thus they are given even greater
value. In this way the "profane" acquires a sacred
aspect and everything in the world is seen as
symbolizing something on high.

There is much to be said for such an analysis, but
the distinctions on which it is based are not as sharp
as Scholem would like us to believe. First of all,
symbols are not "intuitively understood all at once--or
not at all" unless one wishes to make this true by
definition. And in the second place, the inexpressible
is also the subject of much allegorization. Truth-
fully, one should not divide things into the expres-
sible and the inexpressible, for something can be said
about all spiritual realities and yet there is a re-
mainder in each case that cannot be expressed. Obviously, the higher one goes in the spiritual hierarchy
the less one can say. But there is a distinction
Scholem misses which is very important from our viewpoint: the difference between individual symbols and
stories. Examples of symbols, as Scholem understands
them, inevitably involve individual things. But there
does not appear to be any reason for denying that stories too can function symbolically, for they are especially suited to express spiritual growth and degeneration as well as the process by which the world was
manifested.

As to the devaluing (implied by the phrase "empty
shell") of the literal meaning of stories when they are
interpreted allegorically, we can make the following
points. If we decide that a particular Biblical story
is only an allegory, we have in a sense devalued the
events which make it up and the personages involved.
However, if the events never actually occurred, nothing
has really been devalued. In the case of the parables
of Jesus, it is understood that they were invented and
no one worries about their literal sense being
devalued. In the case of other narratives in the Bible
there is great disagreement over whether they were
invented or recount events which actually occurred. It
is our view that many of the stories are not historical

and hence can be properly called allegories. While it is true that some of these stories may contain a kernel of historical truth and that some of the characters in them may be based on people who really existed, this is not enough to deflect us from taking them as allegories. However, even if we agreed that most of the stories to be analyzed recounted historical events faithfully (a matter on which nobody today can have precise knowledge), our treating them allegorically (which does not entail taking them as mere allegories) would in no way devalue them. We would be admitting that the events actually took place but at the same time holding that their spiritual significance lies in what they symbolize.

There is another sense in which it could be claimed that we are devaluing Scripture and it is important enough to be discussed fully. It might be held that we are embarking on a reductionist policy of equating the stories themselves with what we take to be their symbolic meaning. To this charge we must plead "not guilty." As in the case of poems and jokes, explanations of Biblical stories do not constitute the whole of the original article. After all the interpretations are given there is still something left over which cannot be put into words and which, in a sense, strikes the reader directly. We might call it the power of the story, and it would make little sense for us to deny what is so obviously a reality. Besides, it would be equally foolish to deny, what is also obvious, that the stories function on different levels and thus have meanings which are untouched by our symbolic interpretations.

Now that we have analyzed the nature of symbols we can turn to the problem we mentioned at the beginning of the section. For something to <u>function</u> as a symbol (rather than as a mere metaphor or part of a comparison) it must be understood as representing the same or similar things by many people. And here is where we run into trouble in analyzing the symbols of the Bible. What was a symbol to people in a different locality at a much earlier time in history may not be a symbol to us today. Or if something still functions as a symbol today it may indicate something entirely different. An example of the former case is "elder brother." This has no symbolic function in the West today, but it functioned as a symbol in Israel 3000 years ago. An example of the latter case is "snake" or "serpent." At present in the West a snake is a symbol of temptation, sliminess, and evil, or at best a "phallic symbol." But for the ancients it was an ambivalent object, a symbol (among other things) of the earthly, the feminine, healing, prudence, life, immortality,[23] creative energy, death, destruction, and evil. In our study of Biblical symbolism we will have to leave the present-day understanding of people and immerse ourselves in the ancient and traditional understanding of symbols.

e. One Source and Many Sources

It is sometimes argued that we must believe in the literal truth of the stories of <u>Genesis</u> and <u>Exodus</u> because the whole Torah was spoken by God to Moses. The conclusion is a <u>non sequitur</u>, but mentioning this argument provides us with a chance to speak about its premise. One of the quirks of contemporary life is that while scientists are learning more and more about the universe laymen are falling into deeper and deeper ignorance. The gulf as far as knowledge is concerned is widening year by year. While this is generally admitted, very few would think it applied to knowledge about the Bible, yet the gulf in this area is also widening every year. In the last 150 years scholars have found out many important and enlightening facts about the Bible. But unfortunately, very little news of these discoveries has filtered down to laymen. Ignorance of these facts is due mainly to clergymen keeping these discoveries to themselves or choosing to ignore them completely.

It is agreed by most, though not all, Bible scholars that the Torah is a man-made compendium of different sources commonly referred to by the letters J, E, D, and P, standing for Yahwist (Jehovist), Elohist, Deuteronomist, and Priestly, respectively. These were committed to writing between 950 and 550 B.C. with the J source being the oldest. Thus at the beginning of <u>Genesis</u> we find two creation stories (Chapter 1, Verse 1-Chapter 2, Verse 4a, and Chapter 2, Verse 4b-25) which contradict each other in some particulars. The first is from the Priestly source and the second from the Yahwist source. Similar contradictions can be found in the Noah and Joseph stories, and[24] duplicate passages can be found in many stories. Ignoring these findings of Bible scholars has resulted in more of the twisting and turning mentioned earlier. Even some of those who know of these findings and do not ignore them have adopted preposterous explanations of the aforementioned contradictions and duplications, e.g., that the authors of the Bible introduced delib-[25] erate ambiguities into the text. For some reason

12

they have overlooked the obvious explanation that all of the variants of Bible stories were considered sacred by the ancient redactors.

Scholars have also shown that some of the early stories of the Bible are patterned after those of other cultures. Among them are the flood story, the Joseph and Potiphar's wife story, and the baby Moses in the reeds story. None of these discoveries lessens the value of the Torah, for the important thing is the underlying meaning of these stories and not their historical truth.

We must not make the mistake of underestimating the authors of the narratives found in Genesis and Exodus, and assume that they were naively relating stories they took to be historical. They had many purposes in mind and these narratives function on many levels. One purpose was etiological--to explain the origins of things, be they tribes, practices, items of nature, or the general difficulty of living. Another purpose, connected with the first, was to explain the positions of the various tribes of Israel with respect to each other and the non-Israelite peoples around them. Still another purpose was to promote belief in the One God of Creation (monotheism) responsible for every single aspect of the created world as well as the way of life He ordained. And finally, another was to teach certain spiritual truths in a symbolic manner and thus offer a set of directions for the inner journey to God for those with deep enough insight to interpret the symbols.

At any rate, while the whole Torah was not spoken by God to Moses, being instead the result of input from different sources, it was nevertheless inspired by the one ultimate source: God.

f. Literalism and the Modern Mentality

The mentality which says we must take everything in the Bible as the literal truth and the mentality which says the Bible is a collection of falsehoods ("fairy tales") are two sides of the same coin. We are speaking of that more and more worthless coin: the modern mentality. The authors of the Bible would scarcely know what to make of the current controversy. Both sides show that they have very little idea of what the Bible is about.

We may describe the modern mentality as the factualist mentality. Our obsession with "objective facts" is worthless for two reasons. One is that we are not passive in observing creation; we mold the world as much as we perceive it. The second is that even when we turn to scientific instruments to tell us "how the world really is," we run into problems; on the subatomic level we find the observer disturbs the observed in observing it. Thus the realm of facts is one of relative truths. Anything that has to do with temporality and plurality is relative, and this includes morality as well as modern-day science.

Of course, if one has no care for the relative truth one can hardly be expected to care for the absolute truth, and in the case of morality we must reiterate that it is a preliminary for spiritual growth.[26]   But we must not insist too strongly on the acceptance of relative truths and come to treat them as absolutes.

Northrop Frye, in The Great Code,[27] writes that the primary meaning of the Bible is the literal meaning.   But by "literal meaning" he understands the metaphorical sense of the sentences.   He is really getting at the same point we are trying to make in a different way.   He is saying that for the ancients, the most straightforward way of understanding the Scriptures was metaphorically. There is certainly no reason to equate "literal" with "physically descriptive"; this just happens to be part and parcel of the modern turn of mind. We tend to view the ancient writings as expressing the same sort of observation statements with which we are obsessed.[28]   This is analogous to dragging a beautiful jewel through the mud. Then, depending on which side we are on, we either praise the mud-caked jewel as beautiful (which is ludicrous) or point out its ugliness (which is beside the point). We are speaking of the mud of modern understanding which is peculiarly anti-spiritual.

From what has just been said we can understand that the higher truths found in the Bible are not hidden in symbols. Thus, all who would invent reasons for their being hidden are engaged in useless activity. That they appear hidden only shows the blindness and ignorance of present-day humanity. And that the literalistic interpretation of the Bible is taken as the most obvious or natural shows the very same thing.[29]

The use of symbols to express the highest truths is what the Buddhists call an upaya, an expedient means. For one thing, it is difficult to state truths about the suprasensible. One most naturally turns to language that refers to the sensible, and besides, language itself has this bias. Second, using symbols is the best way of preserving the highest truths for the greatest number of people. Symbolic stories will be passed down from generation to generation regardless of whether or not they are understood, even if only in books few read or take seriously. Third, non-linguistic symbols tend to be more suggestive than language. This suits them especially for the expression of the highest truths since the latter can never really be stated precisely, being beyond the distinctions on which language is based. Fourth, and connected with the last, symbols are a help or aid in bringing the understanding along more quickly and permanently than would otherwise be possible. This is especially true when one is dealing with a general audience rather than a select few who have developed enough to understand the highest truths in a more straightforward manner, although even with them, symbols are a help. Finally, nature, from which most symbols are drawn, is an expression of the reality of God. We can say that the whole universe is a theophany or Divine revelation. Should not the plan of nature be such as to suggest our true relationship to God and other metaphysical truths? The most widely acknowledged symbols, which we have already enumerated, are all natural and thus derive from God. In this way, nature becomes a symbol of the supernatural.

As to the hermeneutical principle of our book, it is our view that the same primordial truths, the highest of which are called "metaphysical" in the West, have been expressed variously in different times and places. Thus, the expression of them in Genesis and Exodus is only one case among many, and it is of help in understanding the narratives in these books to consider those in other venerated texts. With the tenets of esotericism in mind, we will not be trying to fit the Biblical tradition into a doctrinal Procrustean bed, but rather indicating basic metaphysical and cosmological doctrines as they appear within the Scriptures. It should be noticed that our interpretations will never contradict or go against the palpable meaning of any Bible passages. And far from "reading things into them," we will be, in Ananda Coomaraswamy's phrase, "reading in them" what they truly contain. Or to use a phrase of the contemporary educator, Harry Broudy, we will be "reading with them," i.e., coming to them with a background understanding of basic metaphysical truths. And we must add that our interpretations will not always be symbolic but some-

times involve noting things presented in a very direct
way which are not seen for what they are by the typical
reader of today.

Notes for Chapter 1

[1] There are certain variations in the exoteric attitude such as viewing oneself as God's child or lover, but the underlying theme is the same.

[2] Chapter 14, Verses 18-21, and Chapter 17, Verses 20-23, and with these in mind Chapter 10, Verse 30.

[3] These passages reflect the original esoteric (and thus initiatic) character of Christianity before it became a source of spirituality for the masses. On this change cf. René Guénon, Aperçus sur l'ésoterisme chrétion (Paris: Gallimard, 1954), Chapter II.

[4] On this subject we read in the Buddhist Dhammapada, "One man on the battle field conquers an army of a thousand men. Another conquers himself--and he is greater." (P. Lal, tr.; New York: Farrar, Straus & Giroux, 1967; p.75.) Rumi devotes a section of the Masnavi to the esoteric understanding of holy war. And, going back to ancient Greece, there is little doubt that the war which Heraclitus glorified was first and foremost the inner one.

[5] The goals of the two rebirths can also be described as building the ego and overcoming the ego. The typical human being of our age hardly possesses an ego and lives his days in inner chaos. Only by over-coming the flesh--which constantly pulls him in different directions and thereby fragments him--can he develop a unity within himself, even if it is a unity which is to be surpassed. Sri Ramakrishna, a Hindu saint of the Nineteenth Century, talked of unripe and ripe egos, and stated that when the ego is ripened it will fall of its own accord.

[6] In Abraham Joshua Heschel's words, "The good is the base, the holy is the summit. Man cannot be good unless he strives to be holy. . . ." (The Circle of the Baal Shem Tov, Chicago: The University of Chicago Press, 1985, p. xxxii.)

[7] As a way of countering evolutionism, such dogmas are quite ineffective, as they concentrate on superficial matters and not the basic idea that intelligence, far from being the end product of the formation of the universe, was there at the very beginning.

[8] On this subject see Frithjof Schuon's "The Two Paradises" in Islam and the Perennial Philosophy (World

17

of Islam Festival Publishing Company, 1976), and his "Alternations in Semitic Monotheism" in Studies in Comparative Religion, Summer 1977.

[9] The Christian form of this belief is typically buttressed by a reference to the Gospel formulation "I am the way, the truth and the life." Unfortunately, this statement is not understood rightly. Jesus can be described in this way because he is an example of what in esoteric doctrine is called "Universal Man," of which we will have more to say in Chapter 11. But that is not to say that one can reach God only through the person of Jesus.

[10] The same sort of thing has resulted from nationalism or culture-identification. Other groups are either slaughtered or taken as slaves to be used like animals.

[11] We mean here to include such traditions as Hinduism, Taoism, Buddhism, and Ch'an (or Zen) Buddhism, which are essentially esoteric in nature.

[12] This view is hardly new, being enunciated in Ancient Rome by those outside of the Judaeo-Christian tradition.

[13] G. K. Chesterton was an especially strong adherent of this idea, and it can be detected, surprisingly, in the writings of Hermann Hesse.

[14] A good rebuttal to the view of the moral West vs. the amoral East is found in Chapter III of S. Radhakrishnan's Eastern Religion and Western Thought, (Oxford University Press, 1959). Frithjof Schuon gives a very clear exposition of the Shinto substitute for morality in Chapter XII of his book In The Tracks of Buddhism (London: George Allen & Unwin, 1968). We very much recommend this chapter to the reader, first because it helps explain our general approach to myths and other spiritual stories, and second because it relates the material we cover in Chapters 10-12 to Shintoism.

[15] Cf. his Mystical Elements In Religion (London: Dent & Sons, 1923), Volume 1, Chapter II.

[16] Some, while not leaving their religion, may join initiatic groups. This will be the case especially where there exist initiatic groups connected with or in the sphere of influence of a particular religion. Others, finding no initiatic groups connected with their religion, will leave it for one to which such

18

groups are connected. Still others, finding a well-developed mystical side to their religion, will pursue that mode of spirituality. Finally, some will leave their religion and join a group belonging to a spiritual tradition which is essentially esoteric. We feel constrained, due to the rise of many aberrant groups in our own time, to say that when we talk of initiatic groups and esoteric traditions we are not referring to what today are termed "cults."

17 We must be careful to distinguish between childishness and the childlikeness attributed to many saints.

18 On First Principles, especially Book IV, Chapters 2 and 3.

19 The Guide of the Perplexed, especially the Introduction and Part I, Chapters 2 and 5.

20 That this was a misunderstanding will be shown in Chapter 10.

21 Cf. Hosea, Chapter 12, Verse 11, Ezekiel, Chapter 17, Verse 2 and Chapter 21, Verse 5, and Proverbs, Chapter 1, Verse 6, all cited by Maimonides.

22 Major Trends in Jewish Mysticism (New York: Schocken, 1954), Lecture I, Section 8.

23 Although this list may seem to be a mélange of disparate elements, many of them are related, as we will go some way toward showing in Chapter 12.

24 In a footnote to "The Forbidden Fruit" in Islam and the Perennial Philosophy, p. 196, Frithjof Schuon writes, "It is not true that the Bible contains divergent 'strata', the one 'Elohist', and the other 'Jehovist'; there is simply a diversity of viewpoint, as in all sacred Scripture." With all due respect it must be pointed out that his positive statement does not support his negative statement. However, if his basic contention is that the so-called "strata" are not in any way opposed to one another when it comes to essential truths, but rather complementary, we can certainly agree with him.

25 Cf. Edmund Leach's "Genesis As Myth" in Myth and Cosmos, ed. by John Middleton (Garden City: The Natural History Press, 1967), "Nobody Lives in the Real World" (Psychology Today, July 1974), and "Anthropological Approaches to the Study of the Bible During the Twentieth Century" in Structuralist Interpretations of

Biblical Myth (Cambridge: Cambridge University Press, 1983). A complete analysis of the correct and incorrect aspects of Leach's general theory and particular applications would require a whole chapter and would be out of place in this book.

26 Maimonides' reference (in The Guide of the Perplexed, Part III, Section 51) to the "ignoramuses who observe the commandments" was, it hardly needs saying, not an indictment of following the Mosaic Law. Rather, it was an indictment of those who would treat the Law as the beginning and end of the spiritual life.

27 New York: Harcourt, Brace, Jovanovich, 1982, Chapter 3, especially pages 59-62. This book is written from a secular or profane point of view, but the author at least recognizes a few truths that escape the many who are trapped in the modern mentality, and his book contains some interesting insights into the Bible.

28 Thus we mistakenly take ancient myths as indicating only the worship of parts and forces of nature. While on this subject we might say that although there is a nature symbolism to many of the ancient myths, there is also a deeper stratum of symbolism which modern interpreters fail to see.

29 The emphasis on the literalistic interpretation of the Bible is not due solely to ignorance. There is a less "innocent" reason which plays a great role. By claiming that all of the Bible stories are literally true (i.e., historically true) Jews and Christians are distancing themselves from and elevating themselves above the pagans and heathens. "Their stories are just stories, but our stories are really true!" Some Biblical interpreters are conscious of such thoughts, but others are only dimly aware of them. This pretense about literal truth is an understandable outcome of the idea of one true religion. But what made Judaism and Christianity preferable to paganism was not the falsity of paganism but its degeneracy. The denial of this view implies that God had abandoned the world until the advent of Judaism.

Chapter 2

The Symbolic Meaning of

Early Biblical History

We will begin our study of the narratives which take us from Adam to Moses by noting a certain cosmological doctrine which, far from being expounded in symbolic fashion, is presented by the Bible in a rather straightforward manner. This doctrine escapes most readers of the Judaeo-Christian tradition because of their linear view of history, a view which is taken for granted in the West. It is rather with what has been called the "cyclical" view of history that we will be dealing.

Perhaps the fullest exposition of the cyclical view is given in Hindu doctrine. We find there first a doctrine of successive ages called the Krita (or Satya) Yuga, Treta Yuga, Dvapara Yuga, and Kali Yuga. In Greek mythology these are termed the Golden Age, Silver Age, Bronze Age, and Iron Age. Although we have not found such a complete theory of ages among their writings, there is little doubt that the Sumerians had one as well. And we also find in Taoist and Ch'an Buddhist writings many references to earlier ages when the level of humanity was higher. As hinted by this last comment these ages represent a degeneration of creation, a progression from order to disorder, a tendency toward chaos.[1] The Golden Age is paradisaical compared to the others, but even it tends to degenerate toward its close. The Iron Age might be called the dark age in comparison to the rest. If the first age is paradisaical, the last, which is our own, is hellish.

According to the second part of the doctrine there is a general destruction or pralaya in the form of a deluge at the end of a complete cycle of ages, and this sets the stage for a new cycle beginning with a new Golden Age. There may also be limited deluges in the course of a cycle. Each cycle is called a manvantara or mahayuga, and fourteen of these (seven descending and seven ascending) are said to make up a kalpa.[2] For our purposes it is not necessary to go beyond this point in the Hindu doctrine. We will say only that within each cycle the ages last for a shorter and shorter time in the ratio 4-3-2-1, and this shortening is also reflected in the lives of humans within the ages.[3]

In the Hindu tradition each cycle is ruled by a Manu who functions as King of the World. There is a primordial Manu (the Adi-Manu) who rules for the whole kalpa, and 14 subsidiary Manus, one for each manvantara, the present one being designated as Manu Vivasvat. This Manu is the Prototype of man and functions as "the primordial and universal legislator" and is thus equivalent to the Greek Minos. He combines priestly and royal functions and brings peace and justice to the world. However, it must be quickly said that Manu Vivasvat should not be viewed as an actual person but as the personification of Divine influence at the beginning of the manvantara.[4]

Of particular interest to us are the correspondences between Manu Vivasvat and Adam, Noah and Moses. Like Manu, Adam is pictured as ruler of the world and as the Prototype of man. Besides this, both Adam and Manu had their wives produced from their ribs.[5] The most obvious correspondence is between Manu and Noah, since both were the survivors of a flood. Manu's connection with Moses might at first seem more tenuous since the latter is not presented as the primordial man. But Moses functions as legislator, and while the royal and priestly functions are split between him and Aaron, we must keep in mind that Aaron is his brother and functions as his alter-ego. And it was Moses to whom God appeared in the theophanies of the bush and mountain. We must also take into consideration that just as Noah escaped drowning in the ark, Moses escaped drowning in the basket which floated on the Nile, and the same Hebrew word, "tebah," is used for both ark and basket. Further, we must not forget the drowning of the Egyptians after the Israelites had crossed through the Red Sea. While none of these matches are exact, they are close enough to be significant, and would seem to indicate a primordial spiritual tradition showing itself in different guises in different places.

Not only are there parallels between Manu and Biblical personages, but also between the doctrine of ages and early Biblical history. At first, in what can be called the Edenic Age, death is unknown and people eat only fruit and seeds. Food is readily available and in general there is no struggle to maintain life. Yet this period is marked by the fall of Adam and Eve which ushers in the Post-Edenic or Ante-Diluvian Age. Even in this age certain conditions continue. Everyone speaks one tongue, lives without laws and is capable of a direct relationship with God. Death is introduced, but people live for hundreds of years. And though people have to till the soil in order to survive, we are given a picture of unity with God and unity among

people.   But there are also indications of a progres-
sive degeneration, such as the murdering of Abel by
Cain.   And by the time of Lamech, several generations
after Adam, life has become very tough indeed.   "When
Lamech had lived 182 years, he begot a son. And he
named him Noah, saying, 'This one will provide us
relief from our work and from the toil of our hands,
out of the very soil which the Lord placed under a
curse'" (Genesis, Chapter 5, Verses 28-29).   Finally,
"The Lord saw how great was man's wickedness on earth,
and how every plan devised by his mind was nothing but
evil all the time" (Chapter 6, Verse 5).   He decided to
blot out all the men and beasts He had created, and
hence the flood.   It is immaterial whether we are to
view this as the end of a whole cycle or just the end
of the Post-Edenic Age, for it is not our contention
that an exact copy of the Hindu system is to be found
in Genesis.

   The flood ushers in the Post-Diluvian Age in which
people live to only 120 years (Chapter 6, Verse 3), eat
other creatures and are given some few laws to live by
(Chapter 9, Verses 1-5).   The direct relationship with
God has been shattered, but a connection between the
heavenly and earthly realms is established by a
covenant whose sign is the rainbow (Chapter 9, Verses
8-17).   The planting of the vine by Noah (Verse 20) is
another indication of a connection between God and man
(wine symbolizing spiritual wisdom), but not as direct
a connection as before.

   Unfortunately, the regenerated human race degenerates once more and people say to each other "Come,
let us build us a city, and a tower with its top in the
sky, to make a name for ourselves; else we shall be
scattered all over the world" (Chapter 11, Verse 4).
The end result of this, and the hallmark of the Post-
Diluvian Age is the appearance of many languages. Here
again we see the movement from unity to disunity, order
to disorder.   The degeneration continues and we meet
with the destruction of the wicked people of Sodom and
Gomorrah (Chapter 19), which is just the flood story on
a small scale, complete with its one surviving family. [6]
We also meet with the first report of idolatry (Chapter
31).

   The Post-Diluvian Age culminates with the slavery
of the Hebrew people in Egypt. Here too we meet with a
picture of the depravity of the human race, especially
in Pharoah's call for the murder of every newly born
male Hebrew child (Exodus, Chapter 1, Verses 15-16).
This is followed by a partial destruction, viz. the
various plagues and the drowning in the Red Sea

(Chapters 7-15) and the ushering in of the Mosaic Age. The Mosaic Age, by virtue of the great number of laws deemed necessary, should be understood as lower or worse than the others. Although the advent of Moses brings with it a regeneration, the Israelites are pictured as backsliding almost from the moment of the Exodus. In any case, the beginning of the Mosaic Age should be seen as paralleling the beginning of the Post-Diluvian Age, the basket of Moses on the Nile being a miniature of the ark of Noah on the flood-waters.[7]

We are not claiming that the ages we have identified in the Bible correspond exactly to the Golden, Silver, Bronze, and Iron Ages. But it is clear that underlying the Biblical narratives is a plan according to which the generation of the world is followed by a degeneration, and then successive eras of regeneration and degeneration which are pictured in a multitude of different ways. In each case, there is a saved remnant, an idea which becomes more pronounced in later Judaism, especially among the Essenes. Although members of the Judaeo-Christian tradition tend to view history as having one beginning and end, certain of their beliefs run counter to this notion. As the Essenes did, most religious Jews and Christians believe in a Judgment Day connected with a great destruction which will bring about God's rule on a renewed Earth (e.g., Revelation, Chapters 20 and 21). This period, during which the saved will be free from death, can easily be viewed as a new Golden Age.

The history of the human race presented in the narrative from the beginning of Genesis to the time of Moses reads like a description of a child growing into adulthood. We begin with orders and punishments and end with a group of laws. There is certainly a symbolism in the notion of childhood, most especially in that it represents primordial purity and innocence. And just as children can be said to degenerate into adults (or in Kant's words, a beautiful butterfly turns into an ugly worm), civilization degenerates down through the ages. But there is a much deeper symbolism to the early historical narratives, and to bring this out we will combine a doctrine of Maimonides with some views of René Guénon.

According to Maimonides[8] the geneologies presented in Genesis are to be seen as spiritual rather than natural. The idea of spiritual geneologies, while not very well known in the West, is commonplace in the East. Thus in the Hindu Upanishads we read in various places that a doctrine or higher knowledge was handed

24

down over the centuries from one person to another. And the annals of Ch'an Buddhism contain at least three different geneologies tracing the teaching of Buddha down to the Ch'an patriarchs in China. This reading of the Biblical narrative is supported by the beginning of Genesis, Chapter 5. In the first few verses it is said that Adam was created in the image of God, and that Adam begot Seth in his own image. As Maimonides points out, this is said only of Seth, and it is through Seth that the lineage of Noah and the patriarchs is traced. Further support for the idea of spiritual geneologies is found in the practice of blessing. Noah blesses his oldest son Japheth, the progenitor of Abraham. Abraham blesses Isaac, Isaac blesses Jacob, and Jacob blesses Joseph. This blessing (berakah) is the imparting of spiritual influence. What we have then is a narrative about an unbroken primordial spiritual tradition—Divine wisdom and influence handed down from generation to generation.[9]

It is here that we bring to bear Guénon's inter-pretation of the symbolism of the ark.[10] In his view the ark serves as the conservator of the tradition in the period between two cycles of ages during which the great deluge takes place. It is at one and the same time the center of creation and the supreme spiritual center which cannot be destroyed and which serves to regenerate the world. We may add to this that the same role is played by the basket of Moses, for it is Moses who is pictured as bringing the law of God to humanity after the Exodus.

It is with respect to the Israelites serving as custodians of this tradition, an ark as it were, that they are called "a light of nations" (Isaiah, Chapter 42, Verse 6). Their custodianship is shown on the tangible level by their carrying around the Ark of the Covenant, the seat of God on earth, i.e., the center of His spiritual influence or Presence on earth.

If our analysis is correct, the picture presented by the early historical narratives of the Bible is of one primordial spiritual tradition serving as a conduit for Divine influence into the world. This influence is personified in the figure of Adam, the Prototype of man. Whether the Adamic tradition goes back to the very beginning of our cycle of ages or represents a subsidiary development, as Guénon insists, is not an important issue as far as we are concerned. And this especially in light of Guénon's claim that the Adamic tradition joined with the main tradition at the time of Abraham.[11] What is important is that it is truly representative of the primordial spiritual tradition

25

and that it presents us with a true picture of where we stand today. Our position, in the latter part of the Kali Yuga, is marked by the spread of mass culture in which the lowest tendencies in people set the standard, by economic considerations overriding all others (to the extent that even the whole of past history is explained on an economic basis as if the primordial spiritual tradition did not exist), by spirituality being reduced to moralism, and by a completely materialistic mode of thought in which only the physical world is recognized and people are seen as mere "hunks of flesh" which are thereby expendable "for the common good." One aspect of the present situation of humanity was summed up by George Orwell in the opening line of a book review: "Modern man is rather like a bisected wasp which goes on sucking jam and pretends[12] that the loss of its abdomen does not matter."

Notes for Chapter 2

[1] If we were to try to fasten on a modern analogy, it would be the increase in entropy in the universe.

[2] One is reminded of the wheels within wheels of Ezekiel's vision (Ezekiel, Chapter 10, Verse 10).

[3] On the shrinking of human ages and other related matters, cf. René Guénon, The Reign of Quantity (Baltimore: Penguin Books, 1972), Chapter 5.

[4] On all of this see René Guénon, Le Roi Du Monde (Paris: Gallimard, 1958), especially Chapter 2, and "Remarques Sur La Doctrine Des Cycles Cosmiques" in Formes Traditionnelles et Cycles Cosmiques (Paris: Gallimard, 1970). The only problem (if we can term it such) with the latter work is Guénon's basing the length of the present manvantara on the reign of the Sumerian king Ziusudra (Xisuthros) whom he equates with Manu Vivasvat. Ziusudra, in Berossus' account of the Babylonian flood narrative, is the equivalent of Utnapishtim in the Epic of Gilgamesh and thus the man who survived the flood. Now Guénon sets his reign at 64,800 years, a figure on which he bases the length of our manvantara. However, Berossus and a second source give his reign as 36,000 years. On the other hand, Berossus gives 64,800 years as the reign of another Ante-Diluvian king named Enmalgalanna. Further, the Sumerian King List begins with the following: "When the kingship was lowered from heaven the Kingship was in Eridu. [In] Eridu A-lulim [became] King and reigned 28,800 years; Alalbar reigned 36,000 years, 2 kings reigned its 64,800 years." [Thorkeld Jacobsen, The Sumerian King List (Chicago: University of Chicago press, 1939), page 71. See also page 76 footnote 34.]

[5] In his role as survivor of the flood his name is Satyavrata.

[6] It is interesting to note in connection with this last remark that just as Noah gets drunk after the flood (Genesis, Chapter 9, Verse 21), Lot gets drunk after the destruction of Sodom and Gomorrah (Chapter 19, Verse 33). Furthermore, the results are somewhat similar. We will have more to say about this in a later chapter.

[7] For the Kabbalistic interpretation of the doctrine of cycles see the "Doctrine of Shemittot" in Gershom Scholem's article "Kabbalah" in the Encyclo-

paedia Judaica (Jerusalem: Keter, 1972), Vol. 10, pp. 579-583.

[8] The Guide of the Perplexed, Part I, Section 7.

[9] The use of the production of generations of people by sexual union as a symbol of the transmission of spiritual wisdom down through the ages should not be surprising. As we shall see in Chapter 12, the production of Eve from the rib of Adam symbolizes a loss of completeness. Thus the union of male and female symbolizes a return to primordial wholeness. It is interesting that at the point of sexual fulfillment one loses one's sense of separateness and incompleteness and attains a sense of unity and nonpurposiveness. One has the experience of dwelling at the center or middle point of the wheel of existence--the point of non-action ("wu-wei" in Taoism), which is one of the aims of spiritual practice. Thus it is that the carrying-on of a spiritual tradition can be symbolized by a history of people produced through sexual union.

[10] Le Roi du Monde, Chapter XI, page 91.

[11] See Le Roi du Monde, Chapter VI. According to Guénon the central primordial tradition entered and thereby legitimated the Adamic tradition in the person of Melchizedek (Genesis, Chapter 14) whom he equates with Manu Vivasvat. We will say here only that his views are problematic on a number of accounts but worth consideration nevertheless.

[12] An Age Like This, ed. by S. Orwell and I. Angus (New York: Harcourt, Brace, Jovanovich, 1968), page 154.

Chapter 3

Cain and Abel

In Chapter 4 of <u>Genesis</u> we are faced with one of those stories which, when taken historically, is unacceptable.[1] The main theme of the story is God's preference for Abel. No reason is given for this preference, and commentators who have wrestled with this story have attempted to make up for this deficiency. The end result has been a rewriting of the story rather than an explanation of it. On the other hand, if we go below the surface of the literal meaning we find that the story makes perfect sense as it stands, and has great heuristic value even though it ends on a negative note. In our own analysis we do not claim to have exhausted its symbolic significance, but we have at least given indications as to the direction its interpretation should take.

Others have looked below the surface of the story of Cain and Abel, but they have not been interested in its spiritual significance. In this connection we must say that while this story may be a reflection[2] of an older one dealing with the rivalry between smiths and herders with a nod to the relatively more regular life of the herders over that of the itinerant smiths, and while the original story may have been used to explain the wandering nature of the smith's work, the story as it appears in <u>Genesis</u> has its own meaning. And it is this meaning we must respect and keep in mind as we interpret it symbolically.

In a well-known passage of the <u>Katha Upanishad</u> the youth Nachiketas is granted three boons by Yama, the God of Death. He chooses as one of his boons knowledge about death. Yama tries to dissuade him from pursuing this topic, offering him instead all the earthly riches he can think of, but Nachiketas sticks to his original request. Of course, in asking about death he is really asking about the possibility of immortality, and the rest of the <u>Katha Upanishad</u> deals with the matter of liberation (moksha). Immortality as understood in the Upanishads is not a matter of living forever after earthly death in our state of human individuality. Rather, it is the realization of our essential unity with God and the sense of eternity which goes along with it. It is thus an immortality within life.

Although this idea of immortality contrasts sharply with the typical religious idea (as we explained in Chapter 1), there are indications in

Genesis and *Exodus* of a view quite comparable to that of the Upanishads. In fact, the early books of the Bible present us with a sort of map to be used for guiding us from our present state of ignorance to the goal of ultimate realization. Of course, we must understand how to read the map if the Bible is to be of use in this regard.

Chapter II of the *Katha Upanishad* begins Yama's explanation with the saying "The better (preferable, sreyas) is one thing and the pleasurable (the agreeable, preyas) another." There are basically two roads we can traverse in this life. One goes in the direction of earthly enjoyments and the other in the direction of the realization of God in our lives. In the story to which we have alluded, Nachiketas picks the latter, for he recognizes that worldly riches are fleeting. It is not merely a matter of *sic transit gloria mundi*. Worldly enjoyments tend to pall in a short time so that any satisfaction we get from worldly pursuits is soon dissipated and new satisfactions must be constantly sought. Besides, the chase after worldly things inevitably brings many troubles in its wake. It must be clear that we are not engaged in moralizing but in stating certain fairly obvious truths.

As there are two paths open to us there are also two inclinations within us which we may call the higher and lower tendencies. These tendencies, which are symbolized by Abel and Cain, stem from our very make-up. We are constituted of body, soul (psyche, anima) and spirit (pneuma). The last is the Divine part of us and may be called the intellect (in the traditional and proper meaning of the word). Plato sometimes calls it the logistikon, Aristotle refers to it as the nous, Kabbalists designate it as the neshamah, and in Hindu doctrine it is called the buddhi. This is the part of us which Aristotle says determines our proper function which involves contemplation (theoria). It is our essence and is for this reason referred to as our heart.[3] As the supra-individual part of us it contrasts with our soul (the seat of our ego-sense and mental functions) and body, which together constitute what has been called our "psycho-physical personality" or individuality. The soul, "caught" between the body and spirit can play the part of devil or angel depending on whether it follows the outward (or downward) pull of the senses or the inward (or upward) pull of the spirit.

The Sufis call the soul enthralled by the lower tendencies the "nafs" or lower soul. It is compared to a mule which stubbornly wants to go its own way and

30

must be disciplined to serve as a vehicle for spiritual advancement. But in the lives of most people this mule is never trained, as the story of Cain and Abel symbolizes.

We must note first of all that Cain is the older of the two brothers. Now while it is true that from the metaphysical point of view the spirit always takes precedence over the soul and body, it is also true that the lower tendencies are the first to develop in a human being and may therefore be termed the oldest. Second, Cain is described as a tiller of the soil, which again suggests the lower tendencies. The higher tendencies, being the last to develop, are aptly symbolized by the younger brother Abel. Besides, he is described as a shepherd, and this has many spiritual connotations including leader, guide and protector.[4]

There is no doubt that the story tells of a preference for the herding over the farming life, but this too has a spiritual significance. A farmer, being sedentary, has a tendency to build up a store of material possessions which entrap him in the lower life. A herder, who must pasture his flocks in different places, cannot afford the luxury of piling up possessions. Further, the spiritual view of life entails seeing ourselves as visitors on this earth, as travellers passing through, and not as sedentary owners of property. Similarly it is said that we must view ourselves as actors on a stage rather than take our worldly doings too seriously. And again, that we must take the part of the guest rather than the host.[5] Only as sojourners can we develop the non-attachment necessary to escape the worldly life and pursue the spiritual life.

While the story shows a preference[6] for the nomadic life, it also, as Guénon points out, symbolizes the swallowing up of the nomadic by the sedentary life, for this is one of the meanings of the slaying of Abel by Cain. "Solidification," Guénon says, is one of the marks of the passage of ages, and it reaches a peak in the last age of the cycle. One aspect of this solidification is the tendency of the sedentary way of life to take over completely so that there is no more room for the nomadic way of life, i.e., life on this earth becomes fixed. It might be thought that in the Twentieth Century there has been a change to a more nomadic existence in that employees are constantly shifted from one locality to another due to the practices of national and international corporations; but appearances are misleading. What we observe is a constant shifting from one fixed location to another.

31

This shadow of the nomadic life carries with it all of the worst aspects of the sedentary life and none of its best aspects. It is another sign of the degenerate nature of our times.

Returning to the central theme of our interpretation we can easily see why God prefers Abel's sacrifice to Cain's. The product of the lower tendencies is worldliness, while that of the higher tendencies is spirituality. But as all those who have pursued the spiritual path know, the lower tendencies are jealous of their prerogatives. Taking the path of worldliness is akin to rowing downstream while taking the path of spirituality analogous to rowing upstream against the current. The first is the path of least resistance and the second of greatest resistance. The pull of the current is constant, and if we are not careful we can be swept downstream. This is indeed the point made by the story of Cain and Abel. The murder of Abel by Cain symbolizes the killing off of the higher tendencies by the lower.

If the lower tendencies prevail within a person he will be condemned to become a "restless wanderer" (Genesis, Chapter 4, Verse 14). We have mentioned that in the pursuit of the lower or worldly things enjoyment fades quickly and the search must be taken up for new forms of pleasure. It is a never-ending quest and accounts for the peculiar frenzied activity that marks our own worldly age. Having persuaded ourselves that "getting there is half the fun," we have embarked on the project of convincing ourselves that there is really no goal and the journey counts for everything. It can be said of us, as it is said of Cain (Chapter 4, Verse 16), that we have settled in the land of Nod--the land of Wandering.[7]

The full verse from which we have just quoted reads: "Since You have banished me this day from the soil, and I must avoid Your presence and become a restless wanderer on earth--anyone who meets me may kill me." On a superficial level the story, as we have said, accounts for the wandering nature of the smith's work: his ancestor was banished from the land for polluting it. But we are interested in the profound meaning of the story, and we thus offer the following interpretation. Anyone who has eschewed the spiritual life has decided to avoid the Presence of God, which amounts to rejecting the Divine Indwelling, for it is the inner presence to which reference is being made. Such a person, estranged from the center of his being, sees himself as subject to harm and death. It is only in his individuality that he is subject to harm and

32

death, but since he tends to identify himself with his body (or at best his psycho-physical personality) he is naturally fearful.

Contrasting with the Cain orientation is the Abel orientation, in which the person identifies himself correctly with the spirit, his true center, which is supra-individual or universal. It is not that he loses his human individuality on the plane of existence, nor even his sense of individuality, although the latter may be interrupted for brief periods. Rather he is no longer attached to his individuality. Such a person "leaves no tracks" on his way through life. He is like a clear window through which the Spirit of God shines. Unconcerned with his safety, what harm can befall him? In the second part of Chapter 50 of the Tao Te Ching we read the following description of the sage, the man of Tao:

> I have heard that one who is a good
> preserver of life does not meet
> tigers or wild buffalos,
> And in fighting is untouched by
> weapons of war.
> There is nowhere for a buffalo to
> butt its horns,
> Nowhere for a tiger to fasten its
> claws,
> And nowhere for weapons to lodge
> their blades.
> How is this?
> Because $_8$in him there is no room for
> death.

Where there is no ego, or better, where the ego has been surpassed, there is no room for death.

In responding to Cain's desperate cry, "The Lord said to him, 'I promise, if anyone kills Cain, sevenfold vengeance shall be taken on him.' And the Lord put a mark on Cain, lest anyone who met him should kill him" (Verse 15). In order to understand the symbolism of the mark of Cain we must keep in mind the differences between the two types of persons we just described. The Abel type, ruled by the higher tendencies, not only cannot be harmed, but also will not harm others since he views others as connected with himself through the Spirit. On the other hand, the Cain type, who is ruled by the lower tendencies, not only can be harmed, but also will be disposed to harm others since he views them only in their mode of individuality and thus as completely other than himself. The mark of Cain is supposed to be protective and so we must ask:

what is it which protects Cain-like people from each other? The answer is at once obvious: morality--the legislation of human activity by God. Morality is what is given (or left) to human beings in their fallen state. Far from being the aim of the spiritual life it is merely a necessary condition of the worldly life if it is to be liveable at all. We can view the mark of Cain as the moral sense or conscience from the inner point of view and as the Law of God from the outer point of view. The mass of mankind must be considered the sons of Cain, as we shall see shortly, and thus they share Cain's mark. The few who are saintly are quite beyond morality, the motivation for their actions springing from quite another source than the constraint of conscience or moral laws.

Following the mark narrative we find information about the descendants of Cain who are described as the bringers of technology to mankind (Verses 21-22). Technology is another necessary concomitant of the fallen state, and it is to be noticed that in stories of almost all cultures the bringing of technology to mankind takes place after[10] and as if to make up for, some spiritual dislocation. Our tremendous dependence on technology makes it difficult to imagine that there was an age when man was such, and his conditions such, that little or no technology was needed for his survival.

While much technology is harmful, some of it is relatively beneficial to mankind. Among other things, Cain's descendants brought us musical technology, and early instruments such as the lyre and pipe are mentioned explicitly (Verse 21).[11] These instruments have a certain spiritual symbolism and, in truth, early technology was always spiritually symbolic in one way or another, thus showing that its introduction was due to Divine influence.[12] And it must be remembered that Cain, although pictured as opposing the Divine order of things, is still presented as being much closer to God (viz., direct contact) than the general run of mankind in our own age. The problem is that as technology has developed in the musical realm and all others the beneficial quality of its products has diminished greatly. Yet every "advance" has been embraced eagerly in the West and the Western world-view is slowly but surely penetrating into the East. This is one of the reasons why we must hold that the mass of mankind are the sons of Cain.

The other reason is bound up with the most well-known of all the passages from the story of Cain and Abel. We are referring to Cain's reply when God questions him concerning the whereabouts of Abel: "I do not know. Am I my brother's keeper?" (Verse 9). This question encapsulates the philosophy of life held by most humans, regardless of their political, religious, or economic posturings. And it cannot be otherwise for Cain-like people. If one sees only the individuality of oneself and others, then one cannot help but treat others in an inferior way, or at least this will be the general tendency.

But not all of mankind are subject to this tendency. The beginning of Chapter 5 of Genesis records the birth of Seth, who, as we mentioned previously, was born in the image of Adam. Side by side with the majority of humanity who are Cain-like, there are beings who have not rejected the Spirit of God and who view themselves as their brothers' keepers. From another angle we can say that side by side with the development of civilization along Cainite lines, the primordial spiritual tradition has survived, even if it has been invisible to most people, and even if it has been subject to great pressures from the forces of "progress."

1 On the outward absurdity of certain Bible stories see Frithjof Schuon's "The Demiurge in North American Mythology" in Logic and Transcendence (New York: Harper & Row, 1975).

2 The name "Cain" probably meant smith. This would help explain why the development of technology was attributed to Cain's descendants.

3 The Biblical injunction to love the Lord "with all thy heart, and with all thy soul and with all thy might" (Deuteronomy, Chapter 6, Verse 5) contains a reference to the three aspects of a human being. Plato, in the Republic, wrongly identifies the spirit as a part of the soul, albeit the highest part. In the Timaeus (69C and D) he refers to it as the immortal part of the soul. In this connection we should say that it is often referred to as the higher soul or higher mind or higher reason or higher intellect, and it is possibly for this reason that the Sufis refer to the nafs (or soul proper) as the lower soul. It would then be contrasted with the ruh or spirit thought of as the higher soul. Plutarch comments on the error of including the spirit (nous) as a part of the soul in his dialogue "Concerning the Face Which Appears in the Orb of the Moon" (Moralia 943A). See also "On the Sign of Socrates" (Moralia 591D-F).

4 On the two inclinations, cf. the comments of Maimonides in The Guide of the Perplexed, Part III, Chapter 22. While he expresses himself in moral terms, it is easy to transpose his comments into our own terms. He notes the teaching that the evil inclination is on the left and the good inclination on the right. Frithjof Schuon (cf. In the Tracks of Buddhism, p. 99) describes the struggle between the higher and lower tendencies as the opposition between knowledge (in the sense of wisdom) and passion.

5 Tao Te Ching, Chapter 69.

6 The Reign of Quantity (Baltimore: Penguin Books, 1972), Chapter XXI.

7 The restless wandering of Cain is to be distinguished from the life led by the herder. Cain represents the "driven" human being, constantly seeking solace in the external world. Abel represents the purposeful human being, moving through the external

world where necessary, but understanding that his true home is not to be found there.

8 This English version is based mostly on the translation of Wing-tsit Chan (Indianapolis: Bobbs-Merrill, 1963).

9 This view of the Law of God is, after all, not so very different from St. Paul's notion of the Law as condemning mankind (Romans, Chapters 3-9) rather than providing a means of being saved. Unfortunately, while Paul was thinking esoterically, he has typically been interpreted exoterically.

10 It is certainly significant that, in many parts of the world, stories describing the transmission of technology to mankind involve the punishment of mankind as well as the "culture hero," e.g., the story of Prometheus, and various trickster stories of the American Indians.

11 That of the pipe is brought out in Rumi's Masnavi and that of the lyre in the sayings of Heraclitus.

12 All ancient stories on the subject trace the original source of technology back to God. That people in our times have seen fit to ignore this is an example of the modern tendency to elevate man or human reason to the status of divinity. The dire results of the human direction of technology are becoming only too apparent.

Chapter 4

The Ark and the Tower

The great regenerators of the earth, such as Noah and Moses, are symbols of the infusion of the Divine influence into the world in times of need. Reading the statement of Lamech about his son Noah (which we quoted in Chapter 2), "This one will provide us relief. . . ." (Genesis, Chapter 5, Verse 25), we cannot help but think of the well-known statement found in Chapter IV, Verses 7-8 of the Bhagavad Gita. It is spoken by Krishna, who is considered to be one of the incarnations of Vishnu (who may be understood as God in this context).

> Whenever there is decay of righteousness and a rising up of unrighteousness, O Bharata, I send forth Myself. For the preservation of good, for the destruction of evil, for the establishment of righteousness, I come into being in age after age.[1]

This comparison takes on added weight when we remember that just before the story of the flood the human race is said to have sunk to a very low level (Chapter 6, Verses 5-6). We must also mention the Mahayana Buddhist description of the journey to spiritual realization as "crossing over the ocean of birth and death," "Mahayana" meaning the great raft. And Buddha himself spoke of the enlightened person as one who has "crossed over" the stream.

In order to better understand the symbolic significance of these bodies of water it behooves us to turn to the Babylonian Epic of Gilgamesh, which contains a prototype of the Noah story. In Tablet XI, Lines 21-27, Utnapishtim, the equivalent of Noah, recounts that he was told the following:

> Man of Shuruppak, son of Ubar-Tutu,
> Tear down [this] house, build a ship!
> Give up possessions, seek thou life.
> Despise property and keep the soul alive!
> Aboard the ship take thou the seed of all living things.[2]

Utnapishtim is being told that for the life of the Spirit he must give up the worldly life, and it is no coincidence that Utnapishtim was subsequently granted immortality by the gods. We are to interpret this immortality in the spiritual sense, rather than the crude spatio-temporal sense.

When Buddha talked about the stream, he meant the stream of life as it is ordinarily lived--the stream of attachments and cravings. The same could be said of "the ocean of birth and death." The ocean must be crossed if we are to attain the sense of eternity in this life. We must note here that in certain traditions paradise is described as an island across the ocean. We will discuss the idea of paradise more fully in the last chapter, but for now we can say that voyaging across the ocean to paradise symbolizes overcoming our lower tendencies and reaching the center of our being where resides the Divine Presence or Indwelling (the Shekhinah). To use a Buddhist mode of expression, it is to travel from the conditioned world to the unconditioned.

With these ideas in mind we can say that the water on which the ark floated can be understood as corresponding to "the ocean of birth and death." (The waters on which Jesus walked are the very same.) They are the waters of attachment to worldly things and the results of this attachment, which are twofold. On the one hand there are the desires to gain and keep the things to which we are attached. On the other there are the negative emotions which result from not being able to gain or keep these things. Thus we have a turbulent sea of attachments, desires, anger, and all the rest. Life--that is, immortal life in the spiritual sense--is gained only if we can keep from being drowned in this sea of ordinary life.

The ark functions as a symbol on at least three different levels. In the context of the present discussion it symbolizes that by which we can escape being drowned in the lower waters. In Buddhism, the raft to cross the ocean of birth and death is Buddha's Dharma or Teachings. But this is only one manifestation of the primordial spiritual tradition which shows itself in the Bible as well. It is this tradition which is the ark for all people at all times, and it is this tradition which we are presently endeavoring to explain.[3] This very same tradition is the vehicle for spiritual rebirth, and that brings us to the other two symbolic meanings of the ark. The ark is at once the seed or egg of the regenerated world and the regenerated person.

Scholars long ago noted that the flood story is really a creation story (although perhaps it would be better to call it a re-creation story). The idea of the world coming from a cosmic egg floating on the waters is found in many cultures, and in contemporary times this sort of picture is derided because it represents the cosmos as an organism which develops in the way all living beings develop. It is thus considered a reflection of times when people did not know any better. Such views are based on too literal an interpretation of what is essentially symbolic in nature, and they completely miss its significance.

Before we discuss the ark as cosmic egg it will be helpful to talk of the waters on which it floated, for in this context the waters serve to symbolize something different from what was just mentioned. They are the lower waters which were separated from the upper or heavenly waters according to Chapter 1 of Genesis. The word "mabbul," which is translated as "flood" in Chapter 7, Verse 10, actually refers to the heavenly waters. In Hinduism, the two waters taken together are called Prakriti, which is one of the two poles of Universal Manifestation. It is the passive or plastic principle in contrast to the active principle which is called Purusha. In Aristotelian terms they correspond to the pairs Substance (Hyle) and Essence (Eidos), pure potentiality and pure act, and prime matter and the Unmoved Mover.[4] Prakriti is often thought of as made up of two parts--the higher part containing the possibilities of formless manifestation and the lower part containing the possibilities of formal manifestation.[5] In the Enuma Elish they are referred to as the god Apsu--the sweet water--and the goddess Tiamat--the bitter water--who lie together before creation. In the flood narrative, the two, as it were, come together once again, the heavenly waters serving to spiritually regenerate the world.

We mentioned in Chapter 2 Guénon's view according to which the ark served as the conservator of the spiritual tradition as well as the center of creation in the period between two cosmic cycles. It is the latter function which concerns us at present. As the story relates, it contains at least two of every animal, i.e., the seeds of creation. The ark is also a symbol of the Unity of Existence before the creation of the plurality which is our world, although we must say that it is a unity poised on the brink of multiplicity. This can be seen from its shape, which is greater in one direction than another (Chapter 6, Verse 15), and it is for this reason that it can be compared to an egg. The unevenness in shape as compared to a sphere indicates that the central point has been split into two foci. This split in the primordial egg is also represented by the Chinese Yin-Yang symbol, which, though circular, is divided into two parts which, in this context, correspond to the duality of earth and sky which we find in the myths of Greece and the Middle East. In order for creation to proceed, the sky and earth (which symbolize the formless and gross physical worlds) must be separated (or propped apart) to allow room for the atmosphere or subtle realm. In the Enuma Elish this is accomplished by Marduk, and in the Rig Veda (Chapter X, Verse 121) it is brought about by Brahman in the role of Creator who "inhabits" the cosmic egg (Brahmanda) in the person of the Golden Embryo (Hiranygharba--whose realm is properly the subtle.) While this is not the method actually described in the Biblical story (which we will get to shortly), it is possible to view Noah in the role of separator, but only with the proviso that we consider him as a personification of Divine influence and not as a human being.

We have been concentrating on the dimensions of the ark, but something must be said about its structure. This will entail looking at its symbolism from a somewhat different perspective. It is described as having three decks and an opening for daylight near the top (Genesis, Chapter 6, Verse 16). If the ark is really the egg of the world then all of these details must have significance. We must not be lulled into thinking that this is just a typical way of building a sea-going vessel, for no ship that ever sailed the seas was built like the ark.

In order to understand its structure we must note that Prakriti is said to be constituted of three strands (qualities or tendencies) in perfect equilibrium. They are the three gunas-sattva (illumination, the upward tendency) rajas (activity, the expansive tendency), and tamas (darkness or inertia, the downward tendency). Prakriti is completely passive, but under the vivifying influence of Purusha the gunas are thrown into a state of disequilibrium which results in the formation of the world. Now as the waters on which the ark floated are really Prakriti or the feminine pole of creation, we can view the ark or cosmic egg as a production of Prakriti, and its three decks will then correspond to the three gunas. The sunlight shining through the top of the ark after the flood corresponds to the Solar Ray proceeding from Purusha--the Spiritual Sun. Thus, as creation is said to take place due to the influence of Purusha on Prakriti, in the Biblical story it is the result of the influence of sunlight on the contents of the ark.

42

With this in mind we can understand the significance of the two birds which Noah releases from the ark
after it lands but before it discharges its contents.
They are, of course, the raven and the dove (Chapter 8,
Verses 6-8). Much has been made of the personality and
habits of these birds, but as far as their spiritual
symbolism is concerned the only thing that matters is
their colors--black and white. Here again we have the
symbolism of the Spiritual Ray--white--and undifferentiated or prime matter--black.[9] It is worth noting
that in the corresponding section of the Epic of
Gilgamesh three birds are released--a dove, a swallow
and a raven. Now each of the gunas has a color associated with it: sattva--white; rajas--red; and tamas--
black. Swallows come in different colors, but a common
type is brown and orange, and this is close enough to
red. Thus the three birds would seem to correspond to
the three gunas. Whichever version of the story we
choose, the important thing is that the birds are
released just before the ark lands and the world is
repopulated, i.e., just before creation takes place.
In the Biblical version stress is being put on the idea
that creation proceeds from the action of Purusha on
Prakriti. In the version from the Epic of Gilgamesh
stress is being put on the idea that the world is made
up of the three gunas.

As we indicated previously, the ark is also the
seed or egg of the regenerated person. This is shown
by the use of the number forty in describing the length
of the flood in the J version of the story. Forty
weeks are normally required for the birth of a child
and forty years was considered the length of a generation. Thus the number forty symbolizes a new beginning which fits very well the idea of spiritual
regeneration. The place of rebirth in spiritual
advancement has been noted earlier and in this connection we can regard the outside of the ark as a kind of
womb from which the regenerated person will be born.
The tripartite division of the ark corresponds on one
level to the physical, emotional and mental aspects of
a person. These are related to the part of the body
below the waist, the torso, and the head. However, it
also refers to the three modalities of human existence
which we mentioned in the last chapter: the gross
physical (body), the subtle (soul) and the formless or
universal (spirit).[10] The first interpretation, which
is the one most natural in our own age, shows a preoc-
cupation with the physical modality. And it must be
said that in Western society the emotional and mental
life of people is generally focused on the body, and
the other modalities are in effect not admitted. But
as we have pointed out, in spiritual advancement there

are really two rebirths, and they correspond precisely to the two higher modalities of human existence. These rebirths were the concerns of the initiations into the "Lesser Mysteries"[11] and "Greater Mysteries" at Eleusis in ancient Greece.

The ray of sunlight shining through the top of the ark is, as we have said, the Divine Ray which functions as the center of the person. The first rebirth initiates a movement toward the Ray and the second begins a movement up the Ray to its source. The first involves the engagement of the subtle modality and the second involves working through this modality to engage the formless modality. We could also describe this situation by saying that the Spirit lies dormant or hidden within a person, and his function is to uncover it and trace its path back to God. It involves a winding up of what has been unwound in creation, a retracing of the steps of creation in consciousness. In doing this, a person will break through his individuality (which comprises the first two modalities), and this "liberation" (or "exaltation") of the spirit is described in Hinduism as its upward penetration through the crown of the head (the brahma-randhra), which corresponds to the window near the top of the ark. It is a movement from the manifested world to the domain of the Unmanifest and thus a movement out of the cosmos symbolized by the head.[12]

The completion of the regenerative process is signified by the covenant of the rainbow (Chapter 9, Verses 8-17). We can look upon this story as merely a folk-tale explanation of the existence of rainbows, but its inner meaning is quite profound. The six colors of the rainbow which come out of the white light of the sun are another symbol of creation, comparable to the animals which come out of the ark when the earth has dried. Furthermore, the rainbow reaches from the sky to the earth thus symbolizing the influence of God in the world. The covenant is one of peace between God and creation, and we must attempt to understand what is involved in this peace.

After regeneration, the world is in proper alignment with God, or as we might say, the world is centered in the Divine Presence. Necessarily, human beings are also in their proper relationship with God. This results in an external and internal peace. External in that, when the elements of creation are in their proper relationship to God, they are also in their proper relationship to each other, and this state of affairs may be described as peace; internal in that persons who are in their proper relationship to God are

44

filled with the inner peace of spiritual attainment. It is perhaps not accidental that viewing a rainbow tends to cause us to forget our cares and become more peaceful. And, in light of our interpretation, we can see that there is something after all to the old tale of the pot of gold at the end of the rainbow. That elusive point where the rainbow touches the earth is really the point of intersection of the Solar Ray with our particular state of existence. There, indeed, is a pot of$_3$ gold, but it is not to be found by any earthly route.[13]

According to Chapter 9, Verse 20, Noah is said to have planted a vineyard. Symbolically, this is a reference to a spiritual center. The wine which comes from the grapes is a symbol of the elixir of immortality, which is really Divine wisdom, and the story of Noah's drunkenness (Verses 21-23) must be understood in this light. Noah is pictured as a man who has absorbed the Divine wisdom and is in a state of realization. In this state, which superficially resembles drunkenness, one has risen above the plurality of the manifested world, and views things from "the standpoint of eternity."

There are two passages in the Brihadaranyaka Upanishad which bear on this matter. The first provides a basis for understanding the second.

> For where there is any semblance of duality, then does one smell another, then does one see another, then does one hear another, then does one speak to another, then does one think of another, then does one understand another. But when all has become one's very Self [Atman, God], then with what should one smell whom? With what should one see whom? With what should one hear whom? With what should one speak to whom? With what should one think of whom? With what should one understand whom?
> (II, iv, 14)

> Just as a man, closely embraced by his loving wife, knows nothing without, nothing within, so does this person, closely embraced by the Self [Atman] that consists of wisdom (prajna), know nothing without, nothing within. That is his [true]

45

> form in which [all] his desires are
> fulfilled, in which Self [alone] is
> his desire, in which he has no
> desire, no sorrow.
>
> (IV, iii, 21)[14]

There is also a short section of the Chuang Tzu about the renowned Emperor Yao which is comparable to the section of the Noah story we are discussing:

> Yao brought order to the people of
> the world and directed the government
> of all within the seas. But he went
> to see the Four Masters of the far
> away Ku-she Mountain, [and when he
> got home] north of the Fen River, he
> was dazed and had forgotten his king-
> dom there.[15]

Ku-she Mountain, the land to the north, is none other than the Terrestrial Paradise, which, as we have mentioned, is the center of our world. To visit it is to taste the nectar of immortality, to reach a state of consciousness beyond individuality and duality. It is no wonder that somebody having this realization would appear dazed or drunk, and this whether he has realized his essential unity with God or he has stopped somewhat short of that.

Ham's breaking in on Noah while the latter is drunk and naked symbolizes the worldly breaking in on the spiritual. Perhaps we should say it represents the disrespect of the worldly for the spiritual. The punishment meted out for this offense is that Ham, through his son Canaan, "shall be a slave to his brothers" (Chapter 9, Verse 25). The worldly person is always a slave, a slave to his own desires. This is the inner meaning of Noah's curse.

If we do not accept Noah's drunkenness as a symbol of a spiritual state, what then can we make of the whole story of Noah? Taken literally, it seems that the one man God considered righteous (Chapter 6, Verse 9) turned out to be a drunkard. Here is one more case where a Biblical story calls out to be interpreted symbolically.

If Noah's ark is a symbol of regeneration, the Tower of Babel is a symbol of degeneration. "Babylon" means gate of the god, and the tower referred to in Chapter 11 of Genesis was probably the ziggurat connected with the Temple of Marduk. It was called "Etemenanki," which means house of the foundations of

46

heaven and earth, and was destroyed around 1550 B.C. by the Hittites.

The names "Babylon" and "Etemenanki" are certainly suggestive of a spiritual center, and it would seem that there was at one time such a center in Babylon which subsequently degenerated. This view is compatible with the story in Genesis as long as we date the decay of the center before the building of the tower.[16] The name of the tower indicates that it was considered to be a symbol of the Axis of the World, connecting Heaven with Earth. This Axis is really the Celestial Ray around which the world is manifested, and thus it is the gateway to God. The problematic aspect of the tower is spelled out very clearly in Chapter 11, Verse 3 of Genesis: "They said to one another, 'Come, let us make bricks and burn them hard.'--Brick served them as stone, and bitumen served them as mortar." People in different cultures have used many naturally occurring objects as symbols for the World Axis, including trees, mountains, meteorites, and large rocks. But the Tower of Babel was not a natural object, and as the Biblical story clearly states, it was not constructed of natural objects.

In Verses 5 and 6 we read: "The Lord came down to look at the city and tower which man had built, and the Lord said, 'If, as one people with one language for all, this is how they have begun to act, then nothing that they may propose to do will be out of their reach.'" He then confounds their speech and stops them from building the city (Verses 7 and 8). On a superficial level we can view this as an explanation for the existence of many languages. Also on this level it would seem that God was jealous of what the people of Babylon were doing. If we reject this hypothesis, we will have to look deeper for the significance of this story.

Essentially it involves a reversal of roles. The builders of the tower had taken upon themselves the prerogatives of God. The world axis comes down from God to earth, and thus it is improper for it to be viewed as going in the opposite direction. Any natural object can serve as a symbol for the axis because, as part of God's creation, it can be said to come from God. But as we have already made clear, not only was the tower not a natural object, it was not even constructed of such objects. In short, it was the product of human technology.

The point of the story is that spiritual realization comes from above, or, as we like to say, by the grace of God, and not from below. It is not a product of man's physical or mental activity but something that occurs when man has gone beyond such activity. And here one recalls Chapter 11, Verse 12 of Matthew: "Ever since the coming of John the Baptist the Kingdom of Heaven has been subjected to violence and violent men are seizing it." This is probably a reference to the activities of the Zealots, and as such it expresses the idea that God's reign on earth is not brought about by man, but by God.

When men, following their lower tendencies, turn from their center (which is God) to what makes up their individuality (their egos), the result is not only inner disharmony but outer disharmony as well, for the unity of mankind is a unity through God. Thus God's "punishment" is really the only possible outcome of the actions of the tower builders.

There is also to be seen in this story a reference to the splitting of the primordial tradition and its universal symbolic language. The result is not so much a loss of the tradition as its being expressed in multifarious ways in such a manner as to hide its unity and prevent different aspects of it from being understood in various places. One might also say that it marks the period when the tradition has become hidden or covered, both as a sign of the age and as a means of protection.

Our own time supplies a peculiar twist on the story of the Tower of Babel. Man no longer looks to God for his salvation but seeks it in his own works. As technology advances with its "towers" mankind is becoming further divided. The paradox is that while the methods of communication are being refined more and more, the amount of communication between people is diminishing more and more.

1 Chapter IV, Verses 7-8. Translation by Eliot Deutsch (New York: Holt, Rinehart and Winston, 1968).

2 Translation by E. A. Speiser from Ancient Near Eastern Texts, edited by James B. Pritchard, Third Edition (Princeton: Princeton University Press, 1969), p. 93.

3 In a secondary way a particular spiritual tradition may be considered an ark, and in a tertiary way a particular building, if properly constructed, may serve this purpose.

4 In Taoism they are represented by the Yin-Yang symbol. In Christianity the active and passive poles are signified by the pair Holy Ghost (or Holy Spirit)-Virgin Mother.

5 Cf. René Guénon, Man and His Becoming According to Vedanta, tr. by Charles Whitby (London: Rider & Co.), p. 63, footnote 1.

6 The three realms or worlds, formless, subtle, and gross physical, are called in Hinduism the Tribhuvana: svah (heaven), bhuva (atmosphere or intermediate region), and bhu (earth). These correspond to Beriah (the world of creation), Yetsirah (the world of formation) and Asiah (the world of making) in Kabbalistic doctrine. These worlds seem to be referred to by Maimonides in Part II, Chapter 30 of the The Guide of the Perplexed as the seas, the firmament and what is above the firmament, all of which, he says, come from the primordial "water." The midrashic literature contains many comparisons of the three sections of the tabernacle (described in Exodus. Chapter 25-27) to the three realms (cf. Exodus Rabbah). These views are admirably summarized by Rabbi Manasseh ben Israel in Question 100 of his Conciliator (tr. by E. H. Lindo, New York: Hermon Press, 1972). In his discussion he mentions that the cherubim on the ark which was placed in the holiest part of the tabernacle are often understood as male and female and are taken to symbolize causes and effects. But this is just another way of referring to them as the active and passive poles of creation. Thus the cherubim represented the primordial duality of which we have spoken.

7 This Solar Ray--Buddhi or Universal Spirit--is said to be the first production of Prakriti, but it can be seen as proceeding from Purusha taken as Being--the

49

Principle or source of both Purusha and Prakriti. A detailed explanation of this as well as the character of Purusha's influence on Prakriti will be given in Chapter 10.

[8] An architectural representation of the ark with its opening near the top is the Gothic cathedral with its rose window. The word for the central portion of the cathedral, "nave," derives from the Latin "navis" (ship) and is related to the Old German "naba" (hub). It is from the latter that we derive the word "navel" for the place where the umbilical cord is attached. Thus the nave, like the ark, is at one and the same time the ship to get us across the lower waters, the hub of creation, and that point from which creation proceeds.

[9] In the Yin-Yang symbol the Yin side is black and the Yang side white.

[10] These, in turn, are reflections of the tripartite constitution of the cosmos, to which we have already called attention.

[11] Plutarch (Moralia 943A-B) describes the first death as the dissociation of the body from the soul and spirit (nous) and the second death as the dissociation of the spirit from the soul. We could describe the first death as the overcoming of the body and the second as the overcoming of the soul, but this would be to oversimplify. The symbolism of rebirth is discussed in great detail by Guénon in Chapters XXXII, XXXIII, and XLI of Symboles fondamentaux de la Science sacrée (Paris: Gallimard, 1962). There is also a great deal of information on the two rebirths in his book Aperçus sur l'Initiation (Paris: Éditions Traditionnelles, 1977). Every spiritual initiation involves leaving behind one's old way of life and taking up a new way of life. Put differently, it is dying to one way of life and being born into another. From this we can understand the Gospel saying, ". . . whoever loses his life for my sake shall find it" (Matthew, Chapter 16, Verse 25). Having died to the old life at the time of initiation one receives a new name. The important thing to note about initiatic rebirth is that it marks the beginning of a process, not the end.

[12] Charles Luk describes a Tibetan tantric practice called Pho-wa for opening the Aperture of Brahma on the crown of the head. It involves the repetition of a special mantra as well as visualization. Cf. Secrets of Chinese Meditation (London: Rider & Co., 1964), pp. 198-201.

[13] It is no coincidence that Iris, the goddess of the rainbow, happens to be Juno's messenger and thus comparable to Mercury. Like Mercury she serves to connect the gods to mankind.

[14] *Hindu Scriptures*, tr. by R. C. Zaehner (London: Dent, 1966), pp. 47 and 67.

[15] *Chuang Tzu*, tr. by Burton Watson (New York: Columbia University Press, 1968), p. 34.

[16] A major theme of the Torah and the rest of the Old Testament is the combatting of spiritual degeneration in the form of idolatry. It may well be that Judaism was meant to fill a spiritual void in its part of the world attendant on the decay of a previous spiritual tradition centered in the Sumerian culture. We should not make the mistake of assuming that before the rise of the major Western religions there was just ignorance and superstition. This view, typical of the modern mentality, is actually very far off the mark. It has engendered the notion that the ancients, in their ignorance, worshipped the sun and various divine couples. That the sun may have symbolized God (and not a sun-god) or that certain of these couples may have symbolized the two-fold nature of Prakriti (and not physical waters) hardly enters anyone's mind. A propos of this we can remark that the ancient mysteries are bound to seem like a lot of magical claptrap to those who do not grasp the traditional ideas which provided their basis. If we understand ancient myths and rituals in their lowest possible way, as was already being done 2000 years ago in the Roman Empire, it is not surprising that we should dismiss them as earlier primitive forms of worship that we have outgrown. The Biblical prophets, too, may have underestimated the spirituality of the surrounding cults and overestimated the amount of idolatry. But the despicable practices associated with many of the cults certainly point to degeneration.

Chapter 5

Abraham and Isaac

There are two great stories of yearning in Genesis and both involve the father-son relationship. In one case the son is not yet born and in the other the son is "lost." The first concerns Abraham's wish for a son, and this theme is the subject of many stories which contain spiritual symbolism. Often these stories involve a test of the father and this one is no exception. But in the midst of the Abraham-Isaac story is another--that of Lot and the destruction of Sodom and Gomorrah, and it is to this other story that we will turn our attention first.

Sodom and Gomorrah are, of course, individual towns, but they represent in capsule form the degeneration of the human race. Only Lot was able to escape this downward tendency, much as Noah was the only one to escape this general tendency of his time. The treatment the Sodomites wished to accord the angels who visited Lot is another symbol of the disrespect of the worldly for the spiritual.

Chapter 19 of Genesis contains a rather remarkable story which sheds much light on the symbolism of the whole episode. Lot has invited the angels into his house:

> They had not yet lain down, when the townspeople, the men of Sodom, young and old--all the people to the last man--gathered about the house. And they shouted to Lot and said to him, 'Where are the men who came to you tonight? Bring them out to us, that we may be intimate with them.' So Lot went out to them to the entrance, shut the door behind him, and said, 'I beg you my friends, do not commit such a wrong. Look, I have two daughters who have not known a man. Let me bring them out to you, and you may do to them as you please; but do not do anything to these men, since they have come under the shelter of my roof.' But they said, 'Stand back! The fellow,' they said, 'came here as an alien, and already he acts the ruler! Now we will deal worse with you than with them.' And they

53

pressed hard against the person of
Lot, and moved forward to break the
door. But the men stretched out
their hands and pulled Lot into the
house with them, and shut the door.
And the people who were at the
entrance of the house, young and old,
they were struck with blinding light,
so that they were helpless to find
the entrance.

(Verses 4-11)

We must view this scene as taking place within a
person. The townspeople of Sodom are the lower tendencies of the individual, especially the various desires
which press in around a person. Lot symbolizes the
soul under the influence of the spirit, and the
presence of the angels in Lot's house symbolizes the
presence of the Divine Spirit. It might be thought
that the Divine Spirit is always present in a person
and thus cannot be symbolized as a guest. However,
while the Spirit is always present, it is not always
paid heed. Inviting the angels into his house
symbolizes turning to the Divine Spirit.[1]

Lot's readiness to sacrifice his unmarried
daughters symbolizes the willingness to throw a bone to
one's desires. While still under their sway one cannot
disregard them altogether. But neither can one give in
to them altogether by turning away from the Divine
Spirit, which in this case would be symbolized by
delivering the angels to the crowd. Freeing oneself
from the lower tendencies often involves treading a
fine line between indulgence and denial. Too much
denial at a particular time may lead to a reaction in
the opposite direction and one may end up being swamped
by a flood of desires.

The crowd wants to be intimate with the angels,
and on a literal level, it is of course sexual intimacy
that is meant. But on the symbolic level it is
intimacy between the flesh and the spirit that is
meant, or better, subjecting the fruits[2] of the higher
tendencies to the lower tendencies. We must also
notice the portrayal of a reversal of proper roles.
The flesh wants to take a masculine or active role with
respect to the spirit, whereas in reality the spirit
plays this role in relation to the soul and body.

The townspeople call Lot an alien who is acting
like a ruler. As a newcomer he symbolizes the soul
under the influence of the higher tendencies which
develop later. The men of the town, symbolizing the

54

various desires, are obviously old residents, and to them the higher tendencies are very much alien. These higher tendencies deserve to rule, but, as we mentioned in the case of Cain and Abel, the lower tendencies have had their way too long to give up easily.

The angels' pulling Lot into the house and blinding the crowd symbolizes the truth that as a person turns to the Divine Spirit within, the Spirit will help him fend off his lower tendencies. To put it differently, if a person can give his higher tendencies some rulership over his lower tendencies, the Divine Spirit will add to this rulership. The light that blinds the townspeople is the light of the Spirit, God being the Spiritual Sun.

In the conclusion of the Lot episode, the angels manage to persuade only a reluctant Lot, his wife, and his unmarried daughters (i.e., that in him which is still untouched by worldliness) to flee Sodom (Verses 14-16). This contrasts with the case of Noah in which the whole family was saved before the destruction. It is of note that Lot refuses to flee to the hills, but instead insists on moving to another town named Zoar (Verses 17-22). The reluctance to flee, and the wish to move to another town has its own significance. Lot symbolizes a soul for whom the spiritual tendency is not very strong. What we have is a picture of an indecisive person loathe to give up his former life, and we will find this same picture presented on a larger scale in the story of the fleeing Israelites in Exodus. It seems that no matter how difficult is the life of inner slavery to one's desires and how glorious the spiritual life, most people would rather cling to their old ways. Lot's decision to move to another town is really a decision in favor of what town-life symbolizes--the life of materiality.

The family is told not to look back at the destruction of Sodom and Gomorrah (Verse 17), but, in the most well-known part of the story, Lot's wife does look back and is turned into a pillar of salt (Verse 26). The theme of not looking back when on the spiritual quest and of the attendant effects of looking back is common in spiritual stories, e.g., Orpheus and Eurydice. Often the protagonist is turned into a stone, and we find that it is a chief trick of the devil to turn his charges into stones. In order to fully understand this we must keep in mind Guénon's comments ₃about the solidification of the world in the Iron Age.[3] The picture of the typical human being as a stone is difficult to accept, especially in light of the mania for activity and emotionalism which characterizes our age. Nevertheless, if we consider the main character of inanimate objects and take a closer look at the life of the typical person, we will find that the analogy is not so far-fetched. An inanimate object cannot bring about any change in itself, although it is subject to change as a result of outside forces, and this is exactly the predicament of the typical individual. Sunken in worldliness, taken up with vanity, and subject to his various desires, he is caught in a mechanical, habitual mode of life. The ego-centered life is indeed the life of a stone or pillar of salt. Those living this sort of existence have achieved death in the midst of life. We can describe this state as death with respect to the Spirit, or spiritual death. The destruction of Sodom and Gomorrah is no less than the destruction of the lower tendencies. If we are attached to them, if we must look behind us when fleeing them, then we are incapable of spiritual progress.

The parallel of the destruction of Sodom and Gomorrah with the flood in Noah's time is shown most clearly in Verses 30-35. Lot's daughters are pictured as thinking that the rest of the human race has been destroyed, thus feeling the need for cohabitation with their father. That Lot's drunkenness must not be taken in the same way as Noah's is shown by the fact that, while Noah drinks of his own accord from the produce of his vineyard, Lot is tricked into drunkenness by his daughters.

With the story of Lot out of the way, we will turn our attention to the story of Abraham. It begins with God telling Abram, "Go forth from your native land and from your father's house to the land that I will show you" (Chapter 12, Verse 1). Ordinarily "father's house" would refer to the Divine Realm, but here it is the equivalent of "native land." In the present case, "native land" refers to the manifested world, and "the land that I will show you" to the Terrestrial Paradise, the center of the manifested world. In short, Abram is being asked to make a spiritual journey.

The Lord goes on to say, "I will make of you a great nation, and I will bless you; I will make your name great, and you shall be a blessing. . . . And all the families of the earth shall bless themselves by you" (Verses 2-3). This would seem to indicate that not only is Abram to achieve the Terrestrial Paradise but the Celestial Paradise as well, thus joining Heaven and Earth and acting as a conduit for the Divine influence.

In Chapter 15 of <u>Genesis</u> we find the first mention of God's promise of a son to Abram. The difficulty in understanding the symbolism of Isaac is that he stands for two different things. To begin with, he symbolizes the "eternal youth," and later on he symbolizes the "most prized possession" as well. The eternal youth is on the one hand a symbol of primordial purity, and on the other a symbol of primordial completeness in that he has not yet become a sexual being. By virtue of his attributes we can say he is a symbol of the Divine Presence in the world.[5]

But much happens before Isaac's birth. Chapter 15, besides recording God's promise, also describes a theophany. We are told that Abram divided up some animals, and then at sunset he fell into a sort of trance in which he had a vision of the Lord passing between the parts of the animals. In this vision the Lord repeats His promise and makes a covenant to fulfill His promise. Scholars have pointed out that the action parallels the typical way in which rulers entered into covenants in that age. The weaker would stand between split animals and declare that if he broke the covenant then this, the splitting, should happen to himself. In a reversal of roles, God takes the part of the weaker party, but all of this concerns the literal level of the story. What is of interest in the vision is that "a flaming torch" passes between the parts of the animals. This flaming torch is really the Spiritual Ray of God and signifies Abram's initiation into the higher life or spiritual way.

In Chapter 17 God reminds Abram of the covenant and changes his name to "Abraham". He also orders Abraham to fulfill his side of the covenant by circumcising himself and all of the males in his group. Circumcision on the eighth day after birth is to be a sign of this covenant forever more. It might be thought that all of this should have taken place in Chapter 15, for it is there that Abraham's spiritual rebirth had occurred. However, it happens that Chapter 15 is from the J source and Chapter 17 from the P source. Thus the story in Chapter 17 is really another version of the story in Chapter 15. In the earlier story stress is put on Abram's vision; in the later one stress is put on the symbols of rebirth. The most obvious symbol is the change of name, but circumcision also has this connotation. Besides the fact that it involves the organ of generation, it implies a stripping away of worldliness (the body) by way of getting back to the primordial purity. But as much has been written on this matter we will say no more about it.

Chapter 21 records the birth of Isaac when Abraham is one hundred years old. Starting his second century is also a sign of rebirth, and we may view the birth of Isaac as both the fruit of Abraham's first rebirth and the occasion of his second rebirth. Abraham's yearning for a son is really a symbol of the yearning of a person for the realization of the Divine Presence. In the birth of Isaac he has realized this, or to use other words, he has touched base with the center of his being and has experienced the Terrestrial Paradise. And here we must repeat something we said in another connection. The Divine Presence is constant, but, from the perspective of the ego, it may seem present or absent.

Abraham's spiritual struggle does not end with the birth of Isaac. In the second phase of the story Isaac becomes a symbol of the most prized possession, or, in general, of worldly possessions. More exactly, we should say he becomes a dual symbol. Abraham has already achieved a great deal on the spiritual path, but the question is whether he is willing to settle for the lesser when he has the possibility of achieving the greater. He has realized the Divine Spirit, but it is now up to him to pursue that Ray to its source. Thus, in the story of the proposed sacrifice of Isaac, the person of Isaac symbolizes both the dearest possession and the Divine Presence.

In Chapter 22 of Genesis we read about God's "test" of Abraham, of which much has been written in an emotional vein. We must admit that the story has great emotional impact, and it is meant to deeply affect the hearer. Nevertheless, we must not be carried away by its literal meaning. Rather, the power of the story should serve to reinforce its inner meaning for our lives. On the worldly level the question is whether we are willing to give up our attachment to even our most prized possessions in order to realize God. And we must understand "possessions" in a wide sense to include fame and power as well as the more obvious things. We must note too that it is the attachment which must be given up. Abraham gets to keep his son, but he has demonstrated his lack of attachment. On the spiritual level the question is whether we are willing to settle for second best.

The outcome of Abraham's test is summarized beautifully in Verses 15-18:

> The angel of the Lord called to
> Abraham a second time from heaven,
> and said, 'By myself I swear, the

58

Lord declares: because you have done
this and have not withheld your son,
your favored one, I will bestow My
blessing upon you and make your
descendants as numerous as the stars
of heaven and the sands on the sea-
shore; and your descendants shall
seize the gates of their foes. All
the nations of the earth shall bless
themselves by your descendants,
because you have obeyed My command.'

Much could be said about this quotation, but most
importantly it shows that Abraham has reached the goal
of the second rebirth and thus has achieved the
Celestial Paradise. By realizing God he has joined
Heaven$_6$ to Earth and become a source of blessing to the
world.[6]

Notes for Chapter 5

¹ In reality the ego is the guest of the Spirit, but from the perspective of the ego it appears the other way around.

² Similarly in Matthew: "When you give alms, do not let your left hand know what your right hand is doing" (Chapter 6, Verse 3). Egoism is always ready to spring out and destroy every higher accomplishment.

³ See Chapter 3.

⁴ One's native land may be a symbol of the manifested world or of one's ultimate source, depending on the point of view. From the stance of individuality, which involves ignorance of our true nature, one's native land is the world. But from the enlightened point of view, which involves the realiation of our essential identity with God, one's native land is what Buddhists call the "Pure Land." In essence this is God Himself. There is a Zen koan which illustrates the second point of view. It is the eighth in a collection of one hundred koan titled The Iron Flute (translated by Nyogen Senzaki and Ruth Strout McCandless, Tokyo: Charles E. Tuttle Company, 1961).

> Yun-chu, a Soto master of Chinese Zen, had many disciples. One monk, who came from Korea, said to him, "I have realized something within me which I cannot describe at all." "Why is that so?" asked Yun-chu, "it cannot be difficult." "Then you must do it for me," the monk replied. Yun-chu said, "Korea! Korea!" and closed the dialogue. Later a teacher of the Oryu school of Zen criticized the incident, "Yun-chu could not understand the monk at all. There was a great sea between them, even though they lived in the same monastery."

The last comment is no doubt ironic. But what particularly concerns us is the use of the monk's native land, Korea, to symbolize his ultimate source.

⁵ Philo devoted a whole book, Who Is the Heir of Divine Things, to a discussion of Genesis XV, although it must be said that much of it is taken up with other matters such as his symbolic understanding of Rachel and Leah, the beloved and hated wives of Jacob. Our

views on the symbolism of Isaac are for the most part in agreement with his, for to him Isaac represents the fruits of the higher life: spiritual inspiration and the blessings of heaven. See especially Sections 34-89. His beautiful description of Abraham's state, based on Verse 5, deserves to be quoted:

> For he [Moses] wished to picture the soul of the Sage as the counterpart of heaven, or rather, if we may so say, transcending it, a heaven on earth having within it, as the ether has, pure forms of being, movements ordered, rhythmic, harmonious, revolving as God directs, rays of virtues, supremely starlike and dazzling. (Translated by F. H. Colson, Cambridge: Harvard University Press, 1967, Section 88.)

6 According to the Zohar, Abraham, through his test, successfully balanced in himself the attributes of rigor and mercy which are represented by the left and right sides of the Sefirotic Tree. This is not the place to go into a detailed explanation of these matters. But in the last two chapters we will see how important is the matter of balance in a person if he is to achieve even the first goal of the spiritual life.

Chapter 6

Esau and Jacob

The story of Esau and Jacob is, in a sense, the obverse of the story of Cain and Abel, since the symbolic structure is the same but the outcome is different.

We are told in Chapter 25 of <u>Genesis</u> that Esau and Jacob were twins, with Esau the older one. As is well known, in many cultures there are stories of twin culture heroes, and in some of these the twins oppose each other. But we must say first of all that neither Esau nor Jacob is represented as a culture hero, and second that the symbolic meaning of the story has nothing whatever to do with the culture hero motif.

Verse 27 informs us that "Esau became a skillful hunter, a man of the outdoors; but Jacob was a mild man, who stayed in camp." Isaac may have favored Esau (Verse 28) but God obviously favored Jacob. On a literal level it is difficult to understand why Jacob should be so favored, especially considering the fact that he takes advantage of Esau on two different occasions. But on a symbolic level the story makes perfect sense.

On one level Esau, the man of the outdoors, symbolizes the man of the senses or the man with his attention turned outwards. Jacob, who stayed in camp, symbolizes the man of spirituality or the man with his attention turned inwards. On another level, Esau represents the lower tendencies of a human being and Jacob the higher tendencies. One's higher tendencies keep one focused on the center of one's being, symbolized by the camp. The world, here symbolized by Isaac, favors the lower tendencies. But the Divine Spirit, here symbolized by Rebecca, favors the higher tendencies. We should add that as Rebecca is the mother of Jacob, God is the ultimate progenitor of Jacob and everything else.

The first example of Jacob's taking advantage of Esau is found in the episode of the bread and lentil stew (Chapter 25, Verses 29-34). One day Esau comes into camp famished and demands some of the stew Jacob is cooking. Jacob gives him the stew in exchange for his birthright. Now the birthright involves precedence, and there is no doubt that the world favors the lower tendencies and gives them precedence in human life. Everything is designed to foster and entrap people in these tendencies, and this is more true in our own time than ever before. Esau's "hunger" is merely a symbol of all the lower tendencies. Jacob feeds Esau, giving Caesar his due as it were, but not before exacting an oath which gives precedence to himself. The lesson of this story is that the higher tendencies can take precedence over the lower, not by fighting the latter, but by giving them only what is necessary with the understanding that this is all they will get. We have here a similar situation to the one in which Lot offered his daughters to the townspeople of Sodom.

On another level the birthright symbolizes our rights as children of God. We are all royalty in that we are part of the family of the King of kings. That is to say, we have the eternal within us if only we would recognize its presence and not go through life as beggars. When the lower tendencies have precedence, we live as Esau--a beggar of food; we have, as it were, sold our birthright for some stew. But when the higher tendencies have precedence, we are on our way to claiming our birthright--the complete satisfaction and joy which comes of realizing our essential identity with God.

In Chapter 27 we find the story of the final victory of Jacob over Esau. This is the well-known incident of Jacob and Rebecca's trickery whereby Isaac mistakes Jacob for Esau and gives his blessing to the former. Thus in this episode, besides symbolizing the world, Isaac functions as the transmitter of the spiritual influence he received from Abraham. The most important parts of the blessing are given in Verse 29: "Be master over your brothers" and "Blessed they who bless you." Thus the higher tendencies are given final rulership over the lower, and Jacob has become a source of spiritual influence in the world.

What is most important is not the particular kind of trickery used, but that it is used at all. The devil is full of tricks, but the devil can also be out-smarted by tricks. It is often the case that one must "fight fire with fire," and this phrase has important implications for the spiritual life which would take us too far afield to discuss in this context. But on the matter of trickery, which can be viewed as one species of fighting fire with fire, we can say the following. The world must somehow be made to loosen its hold upon us. We can try to flee the world, but we will most often find that we have taken the world along. It is easy to be outwardly saintly in a cave, but one's inward life may not have changed at all. A better

64

solution, and one which will ultimately have to be tried in any case, is to turn the world against itself.

The dual nature of Isaac, who functions as supporter of worldliness (Esau) and transmitter of spiritual influence, is paralleled by the nature of the world--Maya--which can pull a person down or be a source of blessing. While our birth can be the beginning of a descent into hell, it can also be a chance to ascend the heavens.[1] It is a matter of what we choose to do in the situation in which we find ourselves. The world teaches us ambition and fills us with desire, but it does not specify the object of that ambition or the nature of that desire. It is like an equation containing variables for which we may substitute whatever constants we choose. In the story this is symbolized by Isaac's blindness: as long as he is fed he does not distinguish between those who feed him.

The world also teaches us that if we want to attain anything we must have a great deal of self-control. There is nothing to stop us from applying this teaching to the realm of spiritual advancement. It is a matter of transmuting lower aspirations into higher and then applying the same method, which in the latter case will take the form of fasting in all of its aspects.[2]

While most people substitute worldly constants into the equation of life, there is certainly no constraint in this regard. The deciding factor is always which tendencies have the upper hand. In this story, as opposed to the one about Cain and Abel, the higher tendencies are stronger and prevail. The spiritual nature of the present story is also shown by the method of trickery which Jacob uses--putting on an animal skin. Putting on such a skin is part of a ritual of rebirth in many cultures.[3] Of course, in the present context we are dealing with spiritual rebirth, and the signs of this rebirth are recorded in Chapter 28 of Genesis.

According to Chapter 28, Jacob flees Esau's wrath after obtaining Isaac's first blessing. He does this on the advice of his mother Rebecca (Chapter 27, Verses 41-45), and here too we can discern a symbolic meaning. Once one is settled on the spiritual path one must be careful not to be pulled back to the worldly path. This is what is symbolized by Jacob putting some distance between himself and Esau. At one point in his travels he stops for the night and dreams of a stairway (the Hebrew "sulam" is very close to "shalom," or peace) reaching up to the sky upon which "angels of God

65

were going up and down" and he also beholds the Lord blessing him (Chapter 28, Verses 10-15). This episode is really the indication that he has achieved the goal of rebirth. The stairway connecting the sky and the earth is the Divine Spirit connecting the Terrestrial and Celestial Paradises and the angels symbolize the higher influences in their ascending and descending modes. Jacob has achieved the first stage on the spiritual journey in that he has travelled horizontally to his own true center. He must now travel vertically up the stairway, whose steps indicate higher states of being, to the abode of God.[4] It is also recorded (Verses 16-19) that Jacob, after describing the place as "the gateway to heaven," took the stone he had put under his head before he went to sleep and set it up as a pillar which he anointed with oil. The stone is another symbol of the connecting link between Heaven and Earth.

In Verse 19 we are told that Jacob named the place of his vision "Bethel" or House of God, but it had previously had the name "Luz." Rabbinical tradition held that Luz was the city of immortality in that no one inhabiting the city could die. The spiritual meaning of this is that Luz was considered an inter-secting point of the Divine Spirit and the world, a place where one could achieve a sense of eternity. We might add that the rabbis also held that there was a bone at the base of the spine which was not part of the gross physical body. They called the bone "luz" and believed that it was from this bone that the person was recreated at the resurrection. On the spiritual level it is obvious that this bone of immortality is none other than the center of the person or that point in which the Divine Spirit intersects man.[5]

The final chapter of Jacob's spiritual quest occurs when he is on his way to make peace with his brother Esau. At night and alone he wrestles with an angel until the break of day. He will not let the angel go until he receives its blessing. As a sign of his second and final rebirth the angel says,[6] "Your name shall no longer be Jacob, but Israel, for you have striven with beings divine and human, and have prevailed" (Chapter 32, Verse 29).[7] This verse indi-cates that Jacob has indeed traced the Divine Spirit to its source and has become a link between Heaven and Earth, a source of Divine influence.[8] It is noteworthy that after this incident Jacob is able to enter into a peaceful relationship with Esau. This reconciliation symbolizes the reconciliation of the higher and lower tendencies. After one has realized one's essential identity with God, the lower tendencies are no longer

66

enemies, or better, they cease to be able to cause harm. They have, so to speak, been put in their place.

Much has been written on the subject of spiritual wrestling, and, in a way, it is the topic of this whole study. However, there are two things we can point out about this particular case. As the story indicates, a great deal of determination and perseverance are necessary to achieve the final goal. Further, the injury to Jacob's "thigh" and the dislocation of his hip (Verse 26), besides hinting at the subject of generation, signify that like any birth, this one involves pain. It is the pain involved in total dis-location, i.e., a wrenching of the person out of and beyond the cosmos.

[1] Cf. Al-Ghazzali, The Niche For Lights, tr. by W. H. T. Gairdner (Lahore: Sh. Muhammad Ashraf, 1952), p. 125, ". . . the visible world is, as we have said, the point of departure up to the world of the realm supernal."

[2] Cf. Al-Ghazzali, The Mysteries of Fasting, tr. by N. A. Faris (Lahore: Sh. Muhammad Ashraf, 1968).

[3] Cf. Section 63 of Myth, Legend and Custom in the Old Testament, Volume 1, by Theodor H. Gaster (New York: Harper & Row, 1975).

[4] If the stairway is understood as spiral then each sweep of it will symbolize a higher state of being.

[5] As to why the spiritual center is pictured at the base of the spine and how this doctrine fits in with that of other traditions, see R. Guénon, Le Roi du Monde, Chapter VII, and Symboles fondamentaux de la Science sacrée, Chapter XXXII, "Le Coeur et l'Oeuf du Monde."

[6] The name "Jacob" probably means may God protect and signifies the protection against the lower tendencies God offers to those on the spiritual path. The name "Israel" originally meant may El persist or persevere or prevail. In this passage the name is reinterpreted to refer to the persistence or prevailing of Jacob. In the present context the two meanings are not opposed since the goal of Jacob with respect to God is the exact correlative of the goal of God with respect to Jacob.

[7] He has "striven" with the higher and lower, with Heaven and Earth, in different ways. While fighting the lower tendencies he has held fast to the Spirit. "Can you discipline your physical soul (p'o, anima in the triad anima, animus, spiritus) and embrace the One (the Tao) and never let go?"(Tao Te Ching, Chapter 10).

[8] Cf. Joseph ibn Aknin's view of the symbolism of the wrestling match as mentioned in A. S. Halkin's article "Yedaiah Bedershi's Apology" in Jewish Medieval and Renaissance Studies, ed. by Alexander Altmann (Cambridge: Harvard University Press, 1967), p. 170. Ibn Aknin, like Maimonides, uses the phrase "Active Intellect" to refer to the Divine Spirit.

Chapter 7

Jacob and Joseph

The second great story of yearning in Genesis centers around Jacob and Joseph. As in the case of Abraham and Isaac it is the father who yearns for the son, and in one respect the symbolism is the same. But we must add that the Jacob-Joseph story goes into detail about things only hinted at in the former story. We can also view the Jacob-Joseph story as a combination of the Cain-Abel and Esau-Jacob stories as it contains elements of both. But again we must add that although the ideas are similar they are expressed in different ways or from a different perspective. That certain themes seem to be repeated in the stories we are discussing is one more reason for accepting the interpretations being offered.

Anyone knowledgeable in spiritual matters will perceive readily that the story of Joseph is really the story of the vicissitudes of the Spirit in the world. It might seem as if Joseph is first represented in a bad light in that he is full of pride and thus cannot possibly symbolize the Divine Spirit. But this view goes against the whole flow of the story. In actuality, Joseph is represented from the first as pure of heart, and this characterization follows him throughout the story. He does not <u>claim</u> to be superior to his parents and brothers <u>but</u> merely <u>dreams</u> these things. And all through the story he is put <u>upon</u> by designing persons.

We are told in Chapter 37 of Genesis that Jacob gave Joseph a special coat or tunic (Verse 3). The translation "a coat of many colors" is a guess at the meaning of the Hebrew words. They could also be translated "a coat of many parts," and this does not contradict the first meaning. It is possible that similar garments were used to clothe statues of gods in other cultures, and it is also possible (taking into consideration II Samuel, Chapter 13, Verses 18-19 and Psalm 45, Verses 13-14) that they were used by royalty. Indeed, another possible translation is "ornamented tunic." It matters little which of these translations we accept since they all point to the same thing. However, "coat of many colors" is the most interesting if we view Joseph as symbolizing the Divine Spirit. As we mentioned in the chapter on Noah, the Divine Spirit is often described as a ray of white light which, in the case of the rainbow, is divided into six colors.

69

Joseph's robe and the rainbow are to be seen as comparable.

The other possible translations point to royalty and divinity, and it is in this light that we must understand Joseph's second dream: ". . . this time, the sun, the moon, and eleven stars were bowing down to me" (Verse 9). Besides the Psalms, spiritual writings from around the world testify that everything in the universe "bows down" before God. So again we must conclude that Joseph, the eternal youth, is a symbol of the Divine Spirit which may be "imprisoned" but never killed.

If we view Joseph in this way then we must view Jacob as symbolizing the soul under the influence of the spirit and Joseph's brothers as the lower tendencies. As usual the lower tendencies are quick to defend their influence and oppose anything having to do with the Spirit within man.

In the story, Jacob makes the mistake of sending Joseph out to where his brothers are pasturing their flocks (Verses 12-14). This exposing of the Spirit to the lower tendencies symbolizes, among other things, putting the Spirit on the same level as the lower tendencies. In other words, Jacob's action indicates a kind of spiritual backsliding on the part of the soul in which the life of the Spirit is held to be of no more importance than the life of the senses. The result in the story is that Joseph is stripped of his tunic and thrown into a pit by his brothers who then dip the tunic in animal blood and present it to Jacob as proof that his son has been killed by a wild beast (Verses 18-33). That there are many parallels to these events in other well-known stories is beside the point. What is crucial is the spiritual significance of Joseph's being thrown into the pit. If the pursuit of the Spirit is put on the same level as the pursuit of the objects of desire, there is little doubt that the latter will swamp the former. The result will be to effectively cut one off from the influence of the Spirit. Thus, as far as Jacob is concerned, Joseph might as well be dead.

As the story continues, Joseph is sold to some slave-traders (Chapter 37) and resold to Potiphar in Egypt (Chapter 39). There he meets with a similar fate as we learn[1] from a story based on the Egyptian Tale of Two Brothers[1] (the unmarried one living in the house of the married one). According to Chapter 39, Potiphar's wife becomes enamoured of Joseph and when he repulses her advances she complains to her husband that Joseph has made advances, and Potiphar has him imprisoned. The story is really a duplicate of the first one with Potiphar substituting for Jacob and Potiphar's wife for Joseph's brothers. We may even conjecture that the same motive of jealously is operative since just as Joseph was his father's favorite he has also become the favorite of Potiphar. The only difference is that the reference to the lower tendencies is more explicit in the case of Potiphar's wife, and here we may bring out another aspect of both stories.

The worldly side of a person works to pull every-thing down to its own level, and thus it attempts to mix with the spiritual side in order to dilute and debase it. The external effects of this tendency can easily be seen in our own time. We have witnessed the debasing of religion until it has become a commodity to be hawked by salesmen. In this manner more and more people are enabled to "get religion," but the religion they get is hardly worthy of the name. We can describe the situation more explicitly as the desire of the material to encompass and possess the spiritual, an absolute reversal of how things actually stand.

As we have already mentioned, the Spirit cannot really be harmed, and we find that Joseph suffers no ill effects from his imprisonment. Through his ability to interpret the meanings of dreams he is eventually made a regent in Egypt, and we can see in this story the eventual triumph of the Spirit. Pharoah's dreams about the cattle and the grain and Joseph's interpre-tations of these dreams (Chapter 41) actually relate to previous episodes in the story. In place of Joseph's brothers and Potiphar's wife we have the seven emaci-ated cows and seven shrivelled ears of grain, and in place of Joseph we have the seven healthy cows and seven healthy ears of grain. In Pharoah's dreams the malformed cattle eat the healthy cattle and the mal-formed ears of grain eat the healthy ears of grain (Verses 17-21). Once again we have the theme of the worldly swallowing up the spiritual. Joseph's advice is to store up the Spirit against the predations of the lower tendencies (Verses 33-36). The executor of this plan is the Pharoah who in this part of the story replaces Jacob and Potiphar. The storing of the grain symbolizes the pursuit of the spiritual life, and is quite comparable to the idea of keeping the lamps full of oil in the Parable of the Ten Virgins found in Chapter 25 of Matthew. The emaciated cattle and shrivelled grain which eat and yet remain in their original states are perfect symbols of the lower ten-dencies, and especially of the desires which are never satisfied. The ascendence of Joseph to power in Egypt

71

is a symbol of the ascendence of the Spirit. Of course, it is only from the limited point of view of the ego that the Spirit can appear to be a prisoner. From the point of view of God, the Spirit is always in ascendence.

Once Joseph has become the Pharoah's chief vizier the stage is set for the great reunion of Jacob and Joseph. First his brothers are put in a position of bowing down before him (Chapter 42), signifying the lower tendencies bowing down before the Spirit. (Here we can recall the story in Chapter 7 of Luke in which the prostitute washes the feet of Jesus with her tears and then anoints them with oil. While the two stories are not completely analogous, the main point is the same.) Finally Jacob is reunited with Joseph in Egypt (Chapter 46) but not before he is asked to give up his other favorite son Benjamin (Chapter 43). In this section of the story Jacob takes the part of Abraham and Benjamin the part of Isaac. The question is quite the same as before: are you ready to give up your nearest and dearest to reach God? In this case, Jacob must give up his child to obtain Joseph's food--the non-material sustenance of the Spirit. The emptiness felt by Jacob at the loss of Joseph, the numbness of heart when he hears that Joseph is alive (Chapter 45, Verse 26), and the joy at being reunited with Joseph (Chapter 46, Verses 29-30) are all symbolic. The first signifies the emptiness of a life from which the Spirit, from the ego's point of view, has departed; the second signifies a return to the heart or spiritual center within a person; and the last signifies the spiritual realization of one's essential unity with God.²

[1] James B. Pritchard, <u>Ancient Near Eastern Texts</u> (Princeton: Princeton University Press, 1969), pp. 23–25.

[2] The resemblance between the story of Jacob and Joseph on the one hand and the story of Demeter and Persephone or Kore (which formed the basis of the Eleusinian Mysteries) on the other is quite remarkable. We point this out not to imply that one was influenced by the other but only to show the universality of certain spiritual symbols. And we can take the opportunity to repeat that while stories such as that of Demeter and Persephone have an obvious natural symbolism (in this case relating to planting and harvesting), they also possess an underlying spiritual symbolism.

Chapter 8

Moses and Aaron

The symbolism of the Exodus is so obvious that it is quite well known. But few have discussed the implications of this symbolism or traced its ramifications. Then too, the only commentators to discuss the symbolic significance of the life of Moses in detail are Philo and Gregory of Nyssa.[1] That is not to deny that other commentators have written on one or another aspect of his life, but there remains much that can be said on this matter. We will begin with the overall picture and then get down to particulars. In keeping to our purpose in writing this book, we will dwell on the stories rather than on the laws handed down by Moses.

The flight of the Israelites from Egypt and their subsequent forty years wandering symbolizes a person's spiritual journey. The slavery in Egypt symbolizes inner slavery to the lower tendencies and the forty years wandering represents the time of purification, for as the story shows, it is not all that easy to slough the lower tendencies. The promised land is the Land of God or the Celestial Paradise. When the story is viewed in this way, Moses becomes a symbol of the higher tendencies within a person. Under the guidance of the Divine Spirit, these tendencies lead the person to his ultimate goal. The death of Moses before his people enter the promised land symbolizes the truth that, at the last, all strivings must be given up. It could hardly be otherwise since all desires are burnt up in the heat of the Spiritual Sun.

Quite consistent with this view, though on another level, is the idea that the advent of Moses represents an infusion of Divine influence into the world, an idea to which we alluded in an earlier chapter. And we must admit that, at times, Moses symbolizes the Divine Spirit, especially as he relates to his brother Aaron. It would be foolhardy to expect the person of Moses to symbolize the same thing throughout all the stories connected with the Exodus. Finally, we must also mention the view of Gregory of Nyssa according to which the life of Moses should be taken as a pattern for our own lives.[2] Considering this view we are able to see how Moses can in one place symbolize the higher tendencies and in another the Divine Spirit. While a person is on the spiritual path and striving for the attainment of the spiritual goal he is in much the same state as the majority of mankind, but once he has attained the goal and has "been elevated to divinity," he becomes "an unapproachable sun," to use some phrases describing Moses from St. Gregory's book <u>On the Canticle</u>.[3] He becomes, in other words, a source of Divine light in the world. And this in turn ties in with the symbolism of Moses we mentioned at the beginning of this paragraph.

The story of the Exodus begins with the Israelites in slavery to Pharoah (<u>Exodus</u>, Chapter 1). As Pharoah symbolizes the world we are given a picture of the unavoidable and universal situation of all who are born. Pharoah proceeds to order the death of all newborn Hebrew males. This favoring of the females over the males can be seen as the favoring of the lower tendencies over the higher or of the passive over the active.[4] The pull of the world is analogous to the pull of gravity in that it tends to keep human beings at the lowest possible level.

But the higher tendencies cannot be totally suppressed and they appear in the person of the baby Moses who is set out to float in the Nile (Chapter 2). We could pause here and rehearse the many parallels to this story which exist, including the birth narrative of Sargon the Great, but his would not in any way lessen its spiritual significance. Mention has already been made of the meaning of floating on the waters in Chapter 4. St. Gregory's interpretation reads practically like a Buddhist exegesis (<u>The Life of Moses</u>, Book II, Section 6-9). He refers to "life as a stream made turbulent by the successive waves of passion, which plunge what is in the stream under the water and drown it." The stream is but another symbol of the world. Moses is plucked out of the stream by Pharoah's daughter, but while he is raised by his adoptive mother he is nourished by his true mother (Chapter 2, Verses 7-9). This signifies that our bodily needs are supplied by the world and our higher tendencies are nourished by God. In the end the higher tendencies exert themselves and Moses kills the Egyptian taskmaster. He flees Egypt and takes up the spiritually significant vocation of shepherd (Chapter 3, Verse 1). This sets the stage for his first significant spiritual experience.

St. Gregory is no doubt correct in attributing great importance to this fleeing of Egypt and embarking on the life of a shepherd (Book II, Sections 16-19). It symbolizes a flight from the outer life of the senses toward the inner life of the spirit. And it will perhaps not be assuming too much if we view Moses' father-in-law Jethro, a priest of the Midianites (Chapter 3, Verse 1), as taking the part of the spiritual master and initiator. Once one has turned one's attention inward the immutable Divine Spirit within will show itself. In the story it takes the form of the bush which burns but is not consumed (Chapter 3, Verse 2). Moses sees the bush on Mt. Horeb (Chapter 3, Verse 1), which indicates an elevated or spiritual state. A voice from the bush tells him to keep his distance and to take off his sandals since he is standing on holy ground (Chapter 3, Verse 5). This particular verse has been the subject of many commentaries and the sandals have been taken to symbolize various things. These interpretations are by no means mutually exclusive but rather reveal different aspects of the symbolism of this wonderful story, much in the way polishing by different hands reveals the different facets of a beautiful gem.

In some passages that are quite Platonic, St. Gregory relates the burning bush to Being (God) or that which is self-subsisting and unchanging, and the sandals to nonbeing (the world of the senses) which is changing and exists only by participation in Being. Truth, for him "is the sure apprehension of real Being."

> Sandaled feet cannot ascend the height where the light of truth is seen, but the dead and earthly covering of skins, which was placed around our nature at the beginning when we were found naked because of disobedience to the divine will, must be removed from the feet of the soul. When we do this, the knowledge of the truth will result and manifest itself. . . In the same way that Moses on that occasion attained to this knowledge, so now does everyone who, like him, divests himself of the earthly covering and looks to the light shining from the bramble bush, that is, to the Radiance which shines upon us through this thorny flesh and which is (as the Gospel says) the true light and the truth itself. A person like this becomes able to help others to salvation, to destroy the tyranny which holds power wickedly, and to deliver to freedom everyone held in evil servitude.
> (Book II, Section 22)

We might think at first that St. Gregory is echoing the Platonic idea that we cannot completely appre-

77

hend the highest realities while in our bodies. But if we are to take the last part of the quotation seriously this cannot be his view, for we cannot help others from beyond the grave. By relating the sandals to the skins which were given to Adam and Eve after the fall he is at the same time relating them to those things associated with the giving of the skins: bodily cravings and human mortality. Thus one meaning of the order to remove the sandals is that sense-based desires must be put aside before the activity of the Spirit can be felt in one's life. Indeed, no approach to the Divine Spirit within is possible if we are unwilling to discipline ourselves in this way. The other meaning of the order is that the sandals, as symbols of mortality, are totally incommensurate with the eternality of the Divine.

It is possible to go further along these lines without mentioning the skins. In the first place the sandals are products of human technology and are thus opposed to what occurs naturally--the works of God-- and, as they are man-made, they are also worldly things. The message is that in approaching God we must put aside the things of the world. In the second place, as things created by man, they serve as a symbol for all created things and thus for the world itself. The message here is that in drawing near to the Divine Spirit we must put away the world.

A related but different interpretation is possible if we consider that there are two sandals. Anticipating a later chapter we can say that Moses is being ordered to put away all dualistic thinking. As one approaches the center of one's own existence and thus the center of creation all dualities disappear. If one is unwilling to let go of distinctions such as subject and object, mine and thine, good and bad, then it is impossible to fall under the influence of the Divine Spirit.

Still another interpretation of the verses in question is given by Al-Ghazzali:[5] "I assert . . . that Moses understood from the command 'Put off thy shoes' the Doffing of the Two Worlds, and obeyed the command literally by putting off his two sandals, and spiritually by putting off the Two Worlds." In one passage he describes the "Two Worlds" in three different ways: "The world is Two Worlds, spiritual and material, or, if you will, a World Sensual and a World Intelligential; or again, if you will, a World Supernal and a World Inferior." He seems to be referring to the Archetypal World on the one hand and to the cosmos which is perceived in part by the senses on the other.

While the one is higher than the other, they both proceed from God considered in His highest aspect. As he says, ". . . for this world and the world beyond [the senses] are correlatives and both are accidents of the human light substance, and can be doffed at one time and donned at another." His comment is a reminder of the truism that anything other than God as He is in Himself, no matter how high it may be, is still something less than the Ultimate Reality.[6]

We have yet to remark on the statement in Chapter 3, Verse 5, "for the place on which you stand is holy ground." This would indicate that Moses has reached the Terrestrial Paradise or the center of his being, and thus has reached the goal of his first rebirth. That he has not reached the ultimate spiritual goal is shown in what follows. He asks God for His name (Verse 13) and God replies "Ehyeh-Asher-Ehyeh" and tells Moses to say to the Israelites that Ehyeh sent him to them (Verse 14). Most scholars understand the name to mean I am that I am, or I will be what I will be. We are dealing here with the personal conception of God as Being, the same conception found in St. Gregory's commentary. Thus when God tells Moses to say that Ehyeh has sent him He is really telling him to say that Being has sent him. But this is not the highest conception of God and Moses has not yet had his ultimate spiritual realization.

In his "role" as Being, what more can God say in describing Himself than "I am"? What then is the point of "I am that I am"? Guénon, who presents the best modern commentary on these verses,[7] feels that the "most exact rendering" of the name is "Being is Being." He first points out that any being "confronting himself as it were in order to know himself, duplicates himself into subject and object; but here again the two are one in reality." On the particular matter of God's name he says the following:

> In fact, Being having been postula-
> ted, what can be said of It (and, one
> must add, what cannot but be said of
> It) is first that It is, and then
> that It is Being; these necessary af-
> firmations essentially constitute the
> whole of ontology in the proper sense
> of the word. The second way of en-
> visaging the same formula is to pos-
> tulate first of all the first Eheieh,
> then the second one as the reflection

of the first in a mirror (image of
the contemplation of Being by Itself). . . .

Thus God in describing Himself considers Himself as
subject and object (or attribute) and says first "I am"
and then "Being is what I am." In this way we are
given a picture of the inner life of God, if we may be
permitted to use this expression, as Being contemplating Itself.[8] It must be kept in mind that while we may
consider what is other than ourselves, there is no
other than God, "all beings in so far as they are manifested in Existence" being "really no more than 'parti-
cipations'" in Being. Thus the description of God (as
Being) contemplating Himself is a complete one which
spells out very clearly the difference between God and
man.

According to Chapter 4 of Exodus Moses worries
that the Israelites may not listen to him (Verse 1).
The Lord's reply is to transform Moses' staff so that
when it is thrown on the ground it will turn into a
snake and when it is picked up by its tail it will turn
back into a rod (Verses 2-4). This will serve as a
sign that Moses has been sent by the Lord (Verse 5).
We know from Chapter 7, Verses 10-12 that when the rod
was thrown down and turned into a serpent Pharoah's
magicians performed the same feat with their rods but
Moses' serpent ate the serpents of the Egyptians. Now
the rod and the snake are really equivalent as symbols
to the tree and the serpent in the Garden of Eden. And
as we have reserved discussion of the latter for a
subsequent chapter we will say only a little at this
time. Once God has transformed the shepherd's staff of
Moses (and the fact that it is a shepherd's rod is significant), it is no longer Moses' staff but God's
staff. As such it is a symbol of the Divine Spirit and
thus equivalent to the vertical axis of the cross. In
the hand of Moses it is the royal scepter signifying
his rulership over the Israelites by Divine right.
Moses, through his brother Aaron who, as we said earlier, functions as his alter ego, is priest as well as
ruler and thus exemplifies the ideal of the priest-king
as the Divine center (or place-holder for God) of his
kingdom. The serpent in this instance symbolizes
immortality and thus complements the Divine rod. The
Divine serpent swallows the worldly serpents of
Pharoah's magicians in an incident symbolizing the hegemony of God over the created world. It also signifies the idea that God engulfs the universe which is
but a drop in the Divine ocean.

In a segment whose symbolic meaning is almost the reverse of its literal meaning Moses complains that he is "slow of speech and slow of tongue" and by implication incapable of transmitting God's message to the Israelites (Chapter 4, Verse 10). It is here that God appoints Aaron to be the spokesman for his brother (Verses 14-16). On the symbolic level there is really no lack in Moses. His inability with words first of all refers to the difficulty involved in expressing the nature of spiritual realization. It is one thing to visit paradise and quite another to talk about it. We must remember that the distinctions on which our conceptual frameworks are built tend to merge as we approach the Divine Spirit. Thus the further into the center we go the more difficult it becomes to describe our journey. Then too, spiritual realization is in a sense dumb. It must be experienced to be really understood, words being only of help in leading people to have the experience. It is not so much that nothing descriptive can be said, but that what can be said is of limited value for those who have not yet attained realization. We are thinking of such phrases as "I am that I am" and "Being is Being."

As to the relationship between Moses and Aaron we must keep in mind the statement of Verse 16, "Thus he shall be your spokesman, and you shall be an oracle to him." As an oracle of God Moses' individuality is effectively negated and his voice becomes the voice of God. In other words, for the Israelites he becomes the Divine Spirit. Aaron, the priest, then becomes a mediator or funnel of the Divine influence for the people, and this is indeed the priestly function. One might compare Moses to the sun and Aaron to the moon which reflects the sunlight. While the Israelites cannot look directly at the sun, they can look at the moon which mediates the sun's light. That is to say, while the Israelites are not yet open to receiving the Divine influence directly, they can be uplifted by the mediation of one who is open.

On the level of the individual, Aaron as spokesman symbolizes the outer or external aspects of a person. As older brother he represents the centrifugal tendencies which, as we have said, are the first to develop. And we must remember, it is Aaron who is prevailed upon to construct the golden calf, a symbol of one of these tendencies. Moses, on the other hand, who is "slow of speech," symbolizes the inner aspect of a person. As younger brother he represents the centripetal tendencies which are the last to develop. And finally, in this connection, we can say that Moses portrays the spirit or heart while Aaron depicts the soul which is the seat of the mental processes. The point is that the heart can speak only through the mind.

[1] St. Gregory's symbolic analysis is given in his book The Life of Moses. Philo's symbolic interpretations are not to be found in his book The Life of Moses, but rather in his Questions and Answers on Exodus. In his book On Flight and Finding he discusses the episode of the burning bush, but his interpretation, if not far-fetched, is at best superficial. The Zohar is ostensibly a commentary on the stories involving Moses as well as the rest of the Torah. However, for the most part, it uses the various stories as jumping-off points for expounding its own version of esoteric doctrines, and when it does engage in commentary this is usually of an exoteric rather than an esoteric nature.

[2] The Life of Moses, tr. by Abraham J. Malherbe and Everett Ferguson (New York: Paulist Press, 1978), Book I, Sections 1-15. All subsequent quotations are from this edition of the book.

[3] Ibid., p. 21.

[4] In this regard cf. Philo, Questions and Answers on Exodus, Book I, Section 8.

[5] The Niche for Lights, pp. 121-143.

[6] The Celestial Paradise is symbolized by the sun, and it is said we must go through the door of the sun (the summit of the cosmos) to reach God. On this see our discussion of the ark in Chapter 4 and Ananda Coomaraswamy's "The Symbolism of the Dome" in Coomaraswamy: Selected Papers, Vol. 1, edited by Roger Lipsey (Princeton: Princeton University Press, 1977).

[7] René Guénon, Symbolism of the Cross, tr. by Angus McNab (London: Luzac & Company, 1958), Chapter XVIII.

[8] Such a picture is analogous to Aristotle's description of the Divine Intellect (Nous) contemplating Itself--Metaphysics, Book XII, 1074b34.

[9] We might mention in passing that the source of Moses' power is the Divine Spirit while the source of the magicians' power is most likely the psychic or intermediate world.

Chapter 9

Moses and Pharoah

Chapter 5 of <u>Exodus</u> records the beginning of the great tug-of-war between Moses and Pharoah for control of the Israelites. In symbols it is the battle between the spirit and the body for possession of the soul. As soon as Moses comes to Pharoah with his request that the Israelites be allowed to worship God in the wilderness the battle is joined. Pharoah immediately instructs the taskmasters and foremen to make the work of the Israelites even harder (Verses 6-9). To those on the spiritual path it is well known that in the inner holy war as soon as there is a tug in the direction of God there will be an opposite tug in the direction of the world. The world works like the force of gravity: every attempt to gain freedom by jumping higher is opposed by the forces of slavery pulling us lower. Like gravity, the pull of the world is always present but it is usually unfelt and unnoticed, showing itself only when opposed.[1]

As if in answer to Pharoah's harsh measures God reveals His name to Moses: "I am the Lord. I appeared to Abraham, Isaac, and Jacob as El Shaddai, but I did not make Myself known to them by My name YHVH" (Chapter 6, Verses 2-3). The significance of this little episode must not be overlooked, and Maimonides spends a whole chapter of his <u>Guide</u> on it. He writes:

> All the names of God, may He be exalted, that are to be found in any of the books derive from action. There is nothing secret in this matter. The only exception is one name: namely, Yod, He, Vav, He. This is the name of God, may He be exalted, that has been originated without any derivation, and for this reason it is called the <u>articulated name</u>. This means that this name gives a clear unequivocal indication of His essence, may He be exalted.[2]

The point is that while a name like El Shaddai is descriptive and from a human source, the name "YHVH" is from a non-human source, namely from the Source of everything. Giving the name of the essence is tantamount to transmitting Divine power, for in this case we have a real example of the adage, "Knowledge is power." Symbolically, the giving of the name to Moses after his rebuff by Pharoah signifies the granting of Divine influence to help the higher tendencies in their fight with the lower tendencies.³

In the next skirmish of the war Moses' snake swallows the snakes of the Egyptian magicians (Chapter 7, Verse 12), "Yet Pharoah's heart stiffened and he did not heed them, as the Lord had spoken" (Verse 13). The Lord had already said he would harden Pharoah's heart in order to enable Him to show His power (Verse 3), but we must not take this literally. The reaction of Pharoah is the normal reaction of the lower tendencies.

We come now to the episode of the ten plagues starting with the turning of the Nile into a river of blood (Verse 20) and continuing with the frogs, lice, insects, pestilence, boils, hail, locusts, darkness, and death of the first born. There is in this episode something of Dante's descent into the various hells, the recapitulation of the lower states of existence which a person must go through before his spiritual ascent. And in the <u>Divine Comedy</u> we find Virgil playing a similar role to that of Moses. It is doubtful that one could tie down each of the plagues as specific symbols. However, we can speak of them as a whole with individual references now and then. The plagues symbolize the attack of the higher tendencies on the lower tendencies under the guidance of the Divine Spirit. The lower tendencies fall into two categories: the lusts for worldly things and the negative emotions such as fear, anger and jealousy. There are also two ways of dealing with these tendencies: education and abstinence, the first being preparatory for the second. The former is symbolized by the plagues and the latter by the wandering in the wilderness.

It is almost a truism that if one finds nothing wrong with the lower tendencies one will do nothing about them. The plagues symbolize the effort to investigate their true nature and ramifications. The lice, boils, and pestilence symbolize the ills to which the flesh is prey, lest we be too concerned with the body. The hail and locusts symbolize the all-consuming nature of desires and negative emotions. The swarming insects indicate the nature of a negative emotion like anger. The turning of the Nile waters into blood symbolizes the polluting nature of the negative emotions. The frogs are a symbol not so easily dealt with, although no doubt St. Gregory is correct in stressing their amphibious nature (Book II, Section 68-72). In the water the frogs are no problem, but during the plague they come up on the land. Bodily desires, when they are confined to serving real bodily needs, are not inimical to a person. But when they forget their rightful place and come to dominate life they are definitely a problem.

The plague of darkness, besides symbolizing the debilitating effects of fear, also stands for the situation of a soul completely given over to the lower tendencies. It wanders in darkness instead of in the light of the Divine Spirit. One could say that this plague summarizes all of the eight we have just discussed.

The last plague, death of the first born, is the most obvious symbol of all and, not surprisingly, it tips the balance in favor of the higher tendencies. The specter of death looms over everyone as much as we may wish to forget it. The last plague puts a question: Do we wish to spend our lives in darkness or in light? It is a matter of choosing the worldly life, which is death, or the spiritual life in which we can attain the sense of eternity. This is the meaning of the well-known passage in Deuteronomy:

> I call heaven and earth to witness against you this day: I have put before you life and death: blessing and curse. Choose life--if you and your offspring would live--by loving the Lord your God, heeding His commands, and holding fast to Him. For thereby you shall have life and shall long endure upon the soil that the Lord your God swore to Abraham, Isaac, and Jacob to give to them.
> (Chapter 30, Verses 19-20)

This matter of choosing eternal life (in the sense indicated) is intimately connected with the method used by the Israelites to save themselves from the effect of the tenth plague: viz., the daubing of their doorposts and lintels with the blood of sacrificial lambs (Exodus, Chapter 12, Verse 7). Blood is the most obvious symbol of life, from which we derive the phrase "life blood." But the doorposts and lintel function symbolically in a way comparable to that of the initiatic ladder and thus signify the World Axis or Divine Spirit. The sacrificial blood of the lambs is the antitype of the influence of the Divine Spirit, which is sometimes symbolized by drops of blood. And we can recall here the blood of the sacrificial bull in Mithraic initiation ceremonies. The flow of this nectar of immortality can be seen as due to the self-sacrifice of the Divine Spirit which must be emulated on an individual level if spiritual advancement is to be possible.[4]

If we wish to obtain the promised land mentioned in the verses just quoted, we must hold fast to God as Moses held fast to his staff, and to do this we must first escape the pull of the lower tendencies. But it is practically impossible to escape the pull of these tendencies on the first attempt. One tries to get free, and one is pulled back. One tries again and perhaps gets a little further, but one is pulled back again. And so it goes, over and over, and a certain tension is built up. One reaches the stage where one can no longer give up the attempts but where one is still not making any progress. At last the energy of the tension is built up to such an extent that the next attempt succeeds, and one is on the road to the promised land. To use a contemporary analogy, we can compare this process to that of getting a rocket off the earth and beyond the earth's gravitational pull into space. The first rockets hardly had enough power to get off the ground. Others were developed which got further and further off the ground but which still fell back to earth. Finally one was developed with sufficient power to overcome the gravitational pull and fly off into space. It takes this much effort to accomplish what is called repentance in the West, and only when this has taken place can an aspirant claim to be on the spiritual path.

But far from being the end it is only the beginning, and any baggage we take with us from our old life hinders us on the way. This is shown by the story of the jewelry which the departing Israelites were given by the Egyptians (Chapter 12, Verse 35). As soon as Moses leaves the people to ascend Mt. Sinai and receive the Ten Commandments the trouble begins. The absence of Moses symbolizes the disassociation of the spirit from the rest of the person. When the action of the spirit (and hence of the Divine Spirit) is interrupted, a person is prey to the pull of the lower tendencies. Thus, in the present story, the Israelites present their jewelry to Aaron for the construction of a calf (Chapter 32, Verses 1-6). The worship of this calf signifies the worship of wealth, and one cannot avoid this sort of backsliding if one carries along the spiritual path any of the baggage of the worldly path. The old cravings must be utterly destroyed, and this is symbolized by the action of Moses in having the calf burnt up, crushed to powder, and swallowed by the Israelites (Chapter 32, Verse 20).

Returning to our account of the Exodus, after Pharoah lets the Israelites go, he has second thoughts and chases after them (Chapter 14, Verses 5-9). This episode vividly portrays the fact that the lower tendencies do not go to sleep once repentance has occurred. They hound a person much as Pharoah hounded the Israelites until the crossing of the Red Sea.[5] This crossing to the other shore is not equivalent to the Buddhist crossing of the ocean of birth and death, although it has some elements in common. The main difference is that, whereas for the Buddhist getting to the other side means reaching the ultimate goal, it obviously does not mean this for the Israelites. Nevertheless, it seems to mark an important milestone on the path in that the Egyptian army is swallowed up in the waters (Chapter 14, Verses 27-28). This signifies a real defeat for the lower tendencies, and if the Exodus itself represents repentance, this last episode symbolizes the first rebirth. The water of the Red Sea functions much as a purifying fire separating the precious metal from the dross, the higher tendencies of the soul from the lower.

Almost as soon as the Israelites begin their trek through the wilderness they begin to complain about their plight. They lack water, and when they discover some at a place called Marah it turns out to be bitter. They grumble to Moses, "So he cried out to the Lord, and the Lord showed him a piece of wood; he threw it into the water and the water became sweet" (Chapter 15, Verse 25). However, the troubles continue in the form of lack of food, and the Israelites begin to wish they were back in Egypt (Chapter 16, Verses 1-3). Following St. Gregory (Book II, Section 132) we must remember that the wandering through the wilderness symbolizes a period of abstinence, a period when a whole former way of living is given up. The adjustment is difficult as the new life seems arid and bitter. But the Lord has ways of sweetening one's plight, as we learn from the example of the wood. The meaning of this becomes clearer in the case of the manna.

The Israelites long for the old life when they "ate their fill of bread" (Chapter 16, Verse 3), but the Lord promises to "rain down bread for you from the sky" (Verse 4). Certainly the new life seems empty and hopeless, but if one perseveres the lord will send heavenly food to replace the earthly. The manna that God sends symbolizes the Divine blessing which fulfills a person completely. Verses 17 and 18 speak to this point: "The Israelites did so, some gathering much, some little. But when they measured it by the omer, he who gathered much had no excess, and he who gathered little had no deficiency." When the Divine influence floods a person's being it is as if all of his desires have been fulfilled, and the joy it brings is not the fleeting joy of earthly satisfactions.[6]

The Israelites are told, "Let no one leave any of it over until morning" (Verse 19), and those who disobey find that it has become rotten with maggots overnight (Verse 20). St. Gregory rightly finds a lesson in this occurrence:

> In this account Scripture after a fashion cries out to the covetous that the insatiable greed of those always hoarding surplus is turned into worms. Everything beyond what they need encompassed by this covetous desire becomes on the next day—that is in the future life—a worm to the person who hoards it. He who hears "worm" certainly perceives the undying worm which is made alive by covetousness.
> (Book II, Section 143)

Evidently St. Gregory's Bible mentioned worms instead of maggots, but the point is the same: Wealth becomes rotten when hoarded. It becomes a source of inner slavery in that it comes to rule us rather than the other way around.

In a parallel story to that of the manna the Israelites cry out again that they lack what they need for sustenance, this time water (Chapter 17, Verses 2-3). The Lord then instructs Moses to go up to Mt. Horeb and strike a certain rock with his staff, and water issues from the rock (Verses 5-6). This water is really no different from the manna and again symbolizes the Divine influence. It quenches the thirst as no earthly water quenches it. The rock from which the water flows is comparable to the rock on which Jacob slept (Genesis, Chapter 28) and as in the former story symbolizes the connecting link between Heaven and Earth. In addition, the rock is situated on Mt. Horeb, the world mountain, which is still another symbol of the Divine Spirit leading up to heaven. In fact, three symbols of the same thing are conjoined in this story: the staff, the rock, and the mountain.

There follows the incident of the war with Amalek in which the Israelites score a major victory. The description of this event is so obviously symbolic that it hardly needs comment. Moses goes up on a hill with

90

the "rod of God" in his hand, and while he holds up his hand the Israelites prevail but when his hand falls through tiredness Amalek prevails. So Aaron and Hur set him on a rock and hold up his hands for the rest of the battle (Exodus, Chapter 17, Verses 8-13). Here again we have the rod, the rock and the mountain mentioned together. As if the meaning of this isn't sufficiently clear Verses 14-16 explain it explicitly:

> Then the Lord said to Moses, "In-scribe this in a document as a remin-der, and read it aloud to Joshua: I will utterly blot out the memory of Amalek from under heaven!" And Moses built an altar and named it Adonai-nissi [the Lord is my banner]. He said, "It means, 'Hand upon the throne of the Lord!'" The Lord will be at war with Amalek throughout the ages.

These statements about the Amalekites are amplified in Deuteronomy Chapter 25, Verses 17-19 where God orders the Israelites to "blot out the memory of Amalek from under heaven."

If we were to take these statements literally we would be led to the conclusion that God was quite bloodthirsty, and indeed many people have claimed on the basis of such passages that the God of the Old Testament is stern and cruel--a God of vengeance. This point of view indicates a complete lack of understand-ing of the inner significance of these passages. There is another section of Deuteronomy which bears on this matter. In Chapter 20 the Israelites are given rules for the conduct of war which preclude the "blotting out" of a people and even prescribe the offer of terms of peace before any attack is begun. But then an ex-ception is made:

> Thus you shall deal with all towns that lie very far from you, towns that do not belong to nations here-about. In the towns of the latter people, however, which the Lord your God is giving you as a heritage, you shall not let a soul remain alive. No, you must proscribe them--the Hit-tites and the Amorites, the Canaan-ites and the Perrizites, the Hivites and the Jebusites--as the Lord your God has commanded you, lest they mis-lead you into doing all the abhorrent

things that they have done for their
gods and you stand guilty before the
Lord your God.

(Verses 15-20)

It is the reason given in the last verse which is
important for our consideration. The Amalekites and
all the other peoples named are symbols of the lower
tendencies which have no place in the promised land,
the land of the Spirit. A person cannot dwell in paradise and still be subject to these tendencies.

The battle against Amalek is really a doublet of
the fleeing from Pharoah. The destruction of the
Amalekites is a doublet of the destruction of Pharoah's
forces in the Red Sea. "The Lord will be at war with
Amalek throughout the generations" means that the Lord
will always oppose the lower tendencies within a
person. Moses, sitting on a rock which is to become an
altar (a throne of God), staff in upraised hand, is a
conduit of Divine influence to his people. Thus it is
really God through the person of Moses who is fighting
against the Amalekites. On the personal level it is a
picture of the Divine Spirit within fighting against
the lower tendencies. When the higher tendencies
weaken, i.e., when the hands fall, a person is no
longer in touch with the Spirit and the lower tendencies prevail. But when the higher tendencies are
revived, i.e., when the hands are held up, the outcome
of the battle is not in doubt.

The wiping out of the Amalekites is obviously related to the swallowing of the remains of the golden
calf to which we have already alluded. Immediately
following the latter occurrence we are told: "Moses
stood up in the gate of the camp and said, 'Whoever is
for the Lord, come here!'" (Exodus, Chapter 32, Verse
26). There comes a point on the spiritual path where
one must make a decision: to go forward or back. One
cannot go in two directions at once, or in the words of
Sri Ramakrishna, one cannot have both "yoga and
bhoga," the life of God and the life of the senses.
The call of Moses to rally to the banner of God is
really the call of the Divine Spirit within to commit
oneself to going forward in the path of abstinence.
More precisely, it is the call for the higher tendencies to separate themselves utterly from the lower
tendencies. And this is another of the meanings of the
saying "Do not let your left hand know what your right
hand is doing" (Matthew, Chapter 6, Verse 3).

Soon after this incident come two appeals by
Moses: "Now, if I have truly gained Your favor, pray

let me know Your ways, that I may know You and continue
in Your favor" (Chapter 33, Verse 13), and "Oh, let me
behold Your Presence" (Verse 18). God answers, "I will
make all my goodness pass before you, and I will pro-
claim before you the name Lord, and the grace that I
grant and the compassion that I show. But. . .you
cannot see My face, for man may not see Me and live"
(Verses 19-20). He goes on, "See, there is a place
near Me. Station yourself on the rock and, as My
Presence passes by, I will put you in a cleft of the
rock and shield you with My hand until I have passed
by. Then I will take My hand away and you will see My
back; but My face must not be seen" (Verses 21-23). In
Chapter 34, Verse 6 we are told that the Lord passed
before Moses proclaiming His name and His compassion.
There are well-known parallels in Greek mythology to
the idea that a human being cannot survive a face-to-
face meeting with the Divine radiance, but there is no
reason to lay great stress on this, especially as the
significance is quite different in the two cases. In
the Biblical case there is no question of harm but
rather impossibility.

Maimonides comments on these passages throughout
Part I of The Guide of the Perplexed:

> Know that the master of those who
> know, Moses our Master, peace be upon
> him, made two requests and received
> an answer to both of them. One re-
> quest consisted in his asking Him,
> may He be exalted, to let him know
> His essence and true reality. The
> second request, which he put first,
> was that He should let him know His
> attributes. The answer to the two
> requests that He, may He be exalted,
> gave him consisted in His promising
> him to let him know all His attri-
> butes, making it known to him that
> they are His actions, and teaching
> him that His essence cannot be
> grasped as it really is.
> (Part I, Chapter 54)

In another place he comments, "In this sense it is also
said: But My face shall not be seen, meaning that the
true reality of My existence as it veritably is cannot
be grasped" (Part I, Chapter 37). And he relates else-
where:

> Scripture accordingly says in this
> passage that God, may He be exalted,

hid from him the apprehension called
that of the face and made him pass
over to something different; I mean
the knowledge of the acts ascribed to
Him, may He be exalted, which, as we
shall explain, are deemed to be mul-
tiple attributes. Whey I say He hid
from him, I intend to signify that
this apprehension is hidden and inaccessible in its very nature.

(Part I, Chapter 21)

The verses we are discussing deal with the supreme
and final realization of Moses, for he has reached the
end of the vertical path to God which he began to climb
at the time of the theophany of the burning bush. It
describes the result of what we have called the second
rebirth: a person's realization of his essential identity with God. This is indicated by Verses 29-30 of
Chapter 34: "So Moses came down from Mount Sinai. And
as Moses came down from the mountain bearing the two
tablets of the Pact, Moses was not aware that the skin
of his face was radiant, since he had spoken with Him.
Aaron and all the Israelites saw that the skin of
Moses' face was radiant; and they shrank from coming
near him." According to this description Moses has
become a medium through which the Divine Sun can be
refracted on earth. This is possible only when one has
reached the height of realization and one's ego, which
blocks the Divine light, has been completely trans-
cended. Moses has become empty of himself and thereby
he has become full of God.

Even so, there is a limit to what can be experienced and apprehended at these heights. God's face,
His essential nature, that Ultimate Voidness or Darkness which is symbolized in Exodus by the Divine cloud,
is beyond all experience and description. This is the
significance, as Maimonides explains so well, of God's
denial of Moses' second request. And St. Gregory, too,
sheds some light on this subject in his comments on
Chapter 20, Verse 21. Speaking of the mind set on the
spiritual path he says the following, quoting from
John, Chapter 1, Verse 19, Exodus, Chapter 20, Verse
21, and Psalm 17, Verse 12:

For leaving behind everything that is
observed, not only what sense compre-
hends but also what the intelligence
thinks it sees, it keeps on penetrating deeper until by the intelligence's yearning for understanding it
gains access to the invisible and the

94

incomprehensible, and there it sees God. This is the true knowledge of what is sought; this is the seeing that consists in not seeing, because that which is sought transcends all knowledge, being separated on all sides by incomprehensibility as by a kind of darkness. Wherefore John the sublime, who penetrated into luminous darkness says, No one has ever seen God, thus asserting that knowledge of the divine essence is unattainable not only by men but also by every intelligent creature.

When, therefore, Moses grew in knowledge, he declared that he had seen God in the darkness, that is, that he had come to know that what is divine is beyond all knowledge and comprehension, for the text says, Moses approached the ark cloud where God was. What God? He who made darkness his hiding place, as David says, who also was initiated into the mysteries in the same inner sanctuary.
(Book II, Sections 163 and 164)

Gregory also shows how the plan of the earthly tabernacle reflects Divine realities: "The curtains divided the tabernacle into two parts: the one visible and accessible to certain of the priests and the other secret and inaccessible. The name of the front part was the Holy Place and that of the hidden part was the Holy of Holies" (Book II, Section 172).

On the granting of the first request Maimonides has something very interesting to say:

For he was told: I will make all my Goodness pass before thee. . . . This dictum--All my goodness--alludes to the display to him of all existing things of which it is said: And God saw every thing that he had made, and behold it was very good. By their display, I mean that he will apprehend their nature and the way they are mutually connected so that he will know how He governs them in general and in detail.
(Part I, Chapter 54)

95

According to this explanation Moses was granted the experience of the unity of Existence. And if we may distinguish between the goodness and the back of God, in the case of the latter Moses was granted the experience of the oneness of Being, one step below the Divine essence.

On the matter of the niche in the rock where Moses positioned himself during the theophany we defer to St. Gregory:

> For the same thing which is here called an opening in the rock is elsewhere referred to as "pleasure of paradise," "eternal tabernacle," "mansion with the Father," "bosom of the patriarch," "land of the living," "water of refreshment," "Jerusalem which is above," "kingdom of heaven," "prize of calling," "crown of graces," "crown of pleasure," "crown of beauty," "pillar of strength," "pleasure on a table," "councils of God," "throne of judgment," "place of name," "hidden tabernacle."
>
> (Book II, Section 247)

In sum, it is the Celestial Paradise, which should not be surprising in light of all we have said concerning the symbolism of the rock on the mountain.

This story of the spiritual progress of Moses does not exactly parallel the story of the progress of the Israelites. If we take the Israelites as symbolizing a person on the spiritual path, the first rebirth, as we have said, occurs at the crossing of the Red Sea, and the second and final rebirth occurs at the crossing of the Jordan River which is described at the beginning of Joshua. That the second crossing is meant to be analogous to the first is shown by the description of the waters of the Jordan piling up to allow the Israelites to walk on dry land (Chapter 3, Verses 14-17). In the two crossings we are thus witnessing the two turning points of the same drama, the human drama of the spiritual journey with all its pitfalls. For the journey to be a success the old ways must be left behind. This is symbolized not only by the swallowing of the Egyptian gold but also by the dying in the wilderness of the generation of the first crossing.[8]

The whole journey can also be likened to approaching and ascending a mountain, and St. Gregory does just this in his discussion of the ascent of Moses in Chapters 19 and 20 of <u>Exodus</u> (Book II, Sections 152-161). Corresponding to reaching the Jordan River would be arriving at the foot of the mountain, and corresponding to conquering the promised land would be arriving at the top. In fact, the two rebirths and corresponding attainments are also symbolized by the structure of the tabernacle. On the one hand we have the Jordan River, the foot of the mountain, and the front part of the tabernacle. On the other we have the promised land, the top of the mountain, and the rear part of the tabernacle. The two parts of this journey are described very beautifully by Origen in his explanation of why the stages of the journey of the Israelites are repeated twice in the Torah:

> The stages are repeated twice in order to show two journeys for the soul. One is the means of training the soul in virtues through the Law of God when it is placed in flesh; and by ascending through certain steps it makes progress, as we have said, from virtue to virtue, and uses these progressions as stages. And the other journey is the one by which the soul, in gradually ascending to the heavens after the resurrection, does not reach the highest point unseasonably, but is led through many stages. In them it is enlightened stage by stage; it always receives an increase in splendor, illumined in each stage by the light of wisdom, until it arrives at the Father of lights Himself. (Cf. Jas. 1:17.)[9]

97

[1] The pull of the world is really the pull of Prakriti, the substance of the world and the passive pole of existence. What we have called a "tug-of-war" is well described by St. Augustine in Book VIII of his Confessions.

[2] Moses Maimonides, The Guide of the Perplexed, tr. by Shlomo Pines (Chicago: The University of Chicago Press, 1963), Part I, Chapter 61. All subsequent quotations are from this translation.

[3] The four letters of the Divine name may well correspond to the "three worlds" of the cosmos plus God (beyond all manifestation) and in this regard cf. the Mandukya Upanishad with its analysis of AUM.

[4] René Guénon has written about the symbolism of blood in "Les fleurs symbolique" which is Chapter IX of Symboles fondamentaux de la Science sacrée. We will have more to say on the significance of sacrificial actions in Chapter 10.

[5] In two articles ["The Reed Sea: Requiescat in Pace," Journal of Biblical Literature, Vol. 102 (1983), pp. 27-35, and "Red Sea or Reed Sea," Biblical Archeology Review, Vol. X, No. 4 (July/August 1984), pp. 57-63] Bernard F. Batto has shown that the reading "Sea of Reeds" for "yam sup" is very questionable. A better translation would be "Sea of the End (of the world)" and the reference is to the primordial chaos. What we have here, in effect, is another creation story similar to the one in which Marduk cleaved Tiamat in two in order to create the cosmos.

[6] In a section of Questions and Answers on Exodus dealing with the sanctuary Philo has the following to say about Divine blessings:

> If, however, thou art worthily initiated and canst be consecrated to God and in a certain sense become an animate shrine of the Father, (then) instead of having closed eyes, thou wilt cease from the deep sleep in which thou hast been held. Then will appear to thee that manifest One, Who causes incorporeal rays to shine for thee, and grants visions of the unambiguous and indescribable things of nature and the abundant sources of

other good things. For the beginning
and end of happiness is to be able to
see God. But this cannot happen to
him who has not made his soul, as I
said before, a sanctuary and altogether a shrine of God.
(Book II, Section 51)

(Translated by Ralph Marcus, Cambridge: Harvard University Press, 1953.)

[7] See Chapter 1, footnote 5.

[8] This dying of the generation of the Exodus also
symbolizes the second death which must occur before the
second and final rebirth.

[9] From "Homily XXVII on Numbers" in Origen, tr. by
Rowan A. Greer (New York: Paulist Press, 1979), p. 253.

Chapter 10

In the Beginning

> When God began to create the heaven
> and the earth--the earth being un-
> formed and void, with darkness over
> the surface of the deep and a wind
> from God sweeping over the water--God
> said, "Let there be light"; and there
> was light.
>
> Genesis, Chapter 1, Verses 1-3

Most English translations of Genesis commence with the words "In the beginning." This is not quite correct and has led to some misunderstandings. A better translation, and certainly less misleading, would be, "When God began to create," for Genesis does not start at the beginning but at some point along the way: the point of Universal Manifestation.

The stages of creation are described differently in the various spiritual traditions, but they have one thing in common: they distinguish between God as He is in Himself, God as He reveals Himself (the Personal or Theistic God of most believers), and God as the Maker of the universe. The latter two are often run together with the second seen as an aspect of the first. The Gnostics, who viewed matter as evil, looked upon the God of Genesis (who they styled the Demiurge, following Plato) as the evil entrapper of the Spirit in matter and thus as completely separate from the true God. This misunderstanding was no doubt due to a failure to view the creation as part of a larger process stemming from possibilities inherent in God (which He made actual by His Will) and completely impelled and infused by Him. It is as if they took one aspect of God, as seen from the human perspective, and considered it as a separate being. But it is impossible to malign the Maker of the universe without at the same time maligning the true God.

God as He is in Himself has been referred to variously as the Supreme Principle or the Unmanifest (Guénon), Nirguna Brahman (Brahman without gunas or unqualified) or Atman (the Self) or Purusha (Hinduism), the Tao (the Way, Taoism), the Void (Buddhism), Eyn Sof (Without End or Infinite, Kabbalism), the Unground (Boehme), and the Ground of Being (Tillich). God as He reveals Himself (or God as He is generally understood in the West) has been[1] called Being (St. Gregory, Al-Arabi, Guénon), Purusha[1] or Isvara or Saguna Brahman

(Brahman qualified, Hinduism), Adam Kadmon[2] (the Primordial or Principial or Universal Man--the Ten Sefirot or first emanations of Eyn Sof, which form the Archetypal World, taken as a whole) or Hokhmah (Wisdom, the second of the Sefirot which proceeds from the first Sefira-Keter, the Crown--considered as the Primordial Ether or the infinite possibilities inherent in Eyn Sof, Kabbalism[3]), and T'ai-i (the Great Unity) or T'ai-chi (the Great Extreme, Taoism). Actually, the Tao Te Ching mentions the nameless Tao and the Tao that can be named. The first corresponds to Nirguna Brahman and the second to Saguna Brahman or Being. Similarly in Hinduism we have references to Purushottama and Purusha, Paramatman and Atman, Parabrahman and Aparabrahman.[4]

God as Creator, as we have said, is often seen as an aspect of God as He reveals Himself. But in this particular capacity we find Him referred to as the Demiurge (Plato--Timaeus 29A), as The Great Architect (Masonry), and as Visvakarman (the All-maker) or Prajapati (the Lord of Creatures[5]) or Brahma (Hinduism).

We can picture the process of creation, which can be considered temporally only from our point of view, as moving from the Void to the Oneness of Being to the Unity of Existence from which the universe proceeds.[6] Using different terminology we can refer to the Unity of Being and the Unicity of Existence, but the signification remains the same. In passing we might note that the Oneness of Being is sometimes pictured as a point which contains all the possibilities of Manifestation, e.g., in the case of Hokhmah.

No doubt there are other ways of describing the process by which the universe is manifested by God, but this one has the virtue of stressing that creation does not take place outside of God. We might say that it represents a certain development within God as long as we do not push that notion too far, for there is no essential change in God with the manifestation of the world, and He remains full and perfect. God is, as it were, playing all the parts in the drama of creation. And by this we do not mean that God becomes Being and then becomes Existence and the world, which would leave us with a pantheistic doctrine. Rather, we must see creation as somehow taking place within God and at the same time infused by God. Perhaps the best image of God's relationship to creation, although it is just an image, is given in the Upanishads. The picture is of a spider spinning and withdrawing its threads (Mundaka Upanishad, I, i, 7). This image may[7] be distasteful to Westerners, but it bears pondering.

102

In order for creation to proceed the original source of creation must bifurcate or polarize, for the distinctive feature of creation is plurality or multiplicity. Thus Being, which is one, must project a second, and these will form a unity of two which we have termed Existence: the active principle and the primordial constituents of the universe.[8] We are presented with this unity at the very beginning of Genesis.

In Chapter 1, Verse 2 we are told that at the beginning of creation the earth was unformed, with darkness surrounding the primordial water and a wind of God blowing over it. Many have recognized that we are here given a description of the primordial chaos, but we must be clear about the meaning of "chaos" in this context. Like many other words of ancient lineage the meaning of this one has become corrupted in modern times. It does not refer to the kind of frenetic and mutually destructive activity observed in such events as riots. Rather, it has the very opposite sense: a cessation of activity, a dissolution into sameness, complete formlessness. Chaos in one's inner life would involve an all-encompassing lethargy and a dissolving of consciousness into oblivion. In short, chaos resembles death rather than life, as strange as this may seem to modern ears. Returning to our subject, we can say that the waters shrouded in darkness are the primordial constituents of the universe in perfect equilibrium. The darkness symbolizes the undifferentiated state of the constituents of the world and signifies that the total of the constituents has no definite qualities.

In searching through ancient Western doctrines we find something similar in the apeiron theory of Anaximander. The apeiron has none of the qualities of the four constituents of the world—coolness, wetness, hotness, and dryness—because it contains them in equilibrium.[9] We have no information from Anaximander on what it is that stirs up the apeiron to produce the cosmos, as he evidently felt it was sufficient unto itself for the task, a mistake on his part. But we are given this information in Verse 1 of Genesis: a wind (ruaḥ) from God. This wind functions as the active principle which throws the waters into disequilibrium with the resultant creation of the universe. But for the process to begin there must be a Divine Impulse from within Being, the Spiritual Sun, and this Impulse is the Word: "Let there be light."[10] From this Impulse comes the first production of the waters under the influence of the wind which is the Light—the Celestial Ray[11]—bringing form out of formlessness.

103

Guénon very perceptively points out that the waters in their chaotic or dark state refer as well to the inner state of a would-be initiate[12] before it has been touched[13] by the spiritual influence of the initiator. Thus each rebirth of the initiate is an inner playing-out of the external drama of creation.[14]

The unity of two that precedes creation, which is described as the wind and waters in Genesis, is called in Hinduism Purusha-Prakriti. Here Purusha corresponds to the wind and Prakriti to the waters. The name "Purusha" is seemingly used to refer to three different things in Hinduism: the Unmanifest, Being, and one of the poles of Existence. However, we are really speaking of different aspects of one subject. The highest signification of "Purusha" is the Supreme Principle. Yet the word "Purusha" means Person, and we find in the Rig Veda X, 90 that the world is created[15] from a part of the body of the Primordial Person. Thus Purusha is also the Principle of Existence. Finally, as Purusha polarizes Itself in order that creation proceed, it is only fitting that It be identified with the active pole of manifestation. As we said before, in the "process" of creation God plays all the parts, and hence all the meanings of "Purusha" merge in the end. In addition to these three meanings of "Purusha" we find that when broken down it signifies the dweller in the city (puri) and as such refers to the Divine Presence inhabiting the body and indeed the world. But this is really only the Unmanifest understood in terms of its relationship with the manifested world.

We have already mentioned that Being must polarize for creation to proceed and we can re-express this by saying that Purusha must project Prakriti, the passive pole of manifestation.[16] The projection of Prakriti is sometimes described as Purusha making Himself into a pair of beings embracing (Brihadaranyaka Upanishad, Part I, Section iv). But as a way of emphasizing that Purusha remains full and perfect through this projection, the creation of Prakriti is sometimes described as coming about by a process of sweating (as in the Brihadaranyaka Upanishad, Part I, Section ii and in the Chandogya Upanishad, Part VI, Section ii).[17] Perhaps the clearest and most complete version of the whole process is given in the Laws of Manu (Chapter I, Sections 5-16). There the self-existent Lord produced water from Himself, deposited seed therein, and the seed became an egg in which He resided. After a year He divided the egg in half and from the halves produced sky, earth and the space between.

We have dwelled at length on the projection of Prakriti from Purusha because it is not mentioned in Genesis; rather, it is presupposed as something already accomplished. At any rate, it is time we said a little more about Prakriti--the waters--and the relationship of Purusha to Prakriti. We indicated in Chapter 4 that Prakriti is constituted by the three gunas--sattva, rajas and tamas--in complete equilibrium. As such it is the passive principle of Existence which must be stirred into disequilibrium by the active principle Purusha--the wind of God in Genesis--in order for the formation of the world to take place.[18] These two-- Purusha and Prakriti--are in no way opposites, but rather complements. Purusha, although active, is said to be unmoving. It works as a magnet would work in drawing iron filings to itself. And here we can see the reason for Aristotle's designation of the active principle as the Unmoved Mover.[19] On the complemen- tariness of Prakriti and Purusha we would allude once again to the passage in the Brihadaranyaka Upanishad in which Purusha becomes "a woman and a man in close embrace" (Part I, Section iv, No. 3), a unity perfectly pictured in the well-known Chinese Yin-Yang symbol. In this case the Yin or passive aspect is equivalent to Earth and is comparable to Prakriti, while the Yang or active aspect is equivalent to Heaven and is comparable to Purusha.[20] The image of the woman and man in close embrace is a reminder that we can describe the Unity of Existence from which creation proceeds as the Primordial Androgyne.

We would be remiss in discussing the creation of the universe as described in Genesis, Chapter 1-Chapter 2, Verse 4a, if we did not comment on the significance of the six days of activity and one of rest. We will begin by noting Philo's views on the significance of the number seven: "So august is the dignity inherent by nature in the number 7, that it has a unique relation distinguishing it from all the other numbers in the decade: for of these some beget without being begotten, some are begotten but do not beget, some do both these, both beget and begotten: 7 alone is found in no such category."[21] The point is that within the decade (which is itself symbolically significant) 7 is the only number neither divisible by any (giving a whole other than itself) nor divisible into any. He goes on to say the following:

It is the nature of 7 alone, as I
have said, neither to beget nor to be
begotten. For this reason other
philosophers liken this number to the
motherless and virgin Nike, who is

105

said to have appeared out of the head of Zeus, while the Pythagoreans liken it to the chief of all things: for that which neither begets nor is begotten remains motionless; for creation takes place in movement, since there is movement both in that which begets and in that which is begotten, in the one that it may beget, in the other that it may be begotten. There is only one thing that neither causes motion nor experiences it, the original ruler and sovereign. Of Him 7 may be fitly said to be a symbol. Evidence of what I say is supplied by Philolaus in these words: "There is, he says, a supreme Ruler of all things, God, ever One, abiding, without motion, Himself (alone) like unto Himself, different from all others."[22]

The idea is that 7 is a perfect number to represent Being, that primal point from which the cosmos springs, the Principle of the active and passive poles of creation.

On the basis of what we have just said we can understand that the first six days of the week represent the six directions in which God manifests the world--the four cardinal points plus above and below. The seventh day represents the center from which manifestation proceeds and thus eternity in the midst of temporality as well. We find a similar symbolism in the six colors of the spectrum which resolve into white light. The Seal of Solomon, now usually called the "Shield of David," which is composed of inverted triangles, is a perfect symbol of the six directions of creation represented two-dimensionally. The center of this symbol corresponds to the center of creation and hence to the seventh day. Finally, the seven days represent the seven cycles of ages or manvantaras which have already occurred in our kalpa.[23]

The point of observing the sabbath should be clear by this time. It involves a return to the central repose, a focusing inward in contrast to the outward expenditure of attention and energy which characterizes the rest of the week. It is a dip in the sea of eternity from which we can return with renewed vigor. Of course, all of this is what the observance of the sabbath should be, and not necessarily what it is for most people. Much the same can be said for making the sign of the cross, a gesture with the same symbolic meaning as observing the sabbath—viz., centering oneself. The vertical axis of the cross symbolizes the Divine Spirit and the horizontal axis symbolizes our particular state of existence (or realm of being). Their point of intersection is the still point around which our world revolves. But how many people in using this gesture are aware of its significance or are affected by it to any degree? All remembrance of God, whether it takes the form of a prayer before meals or sleep or some other form, involves the potential for centering oneself. But whether the potential is actualized in a person's life depends on his or her intentions and receptivity. While a discussion on this subject would take us too far afield, we can say, what is in any case very obvious, that very few people are the least bit affected by activities meant for the purpose of centering them in the Celestial Ray of the Divine Sun.

1 Especially in the Rig Veda, X, 90.

2 In Sufism the equivalent name is "El-Insanul Kamil."

3 Fortunately or unfortunately the various Kabbalists had different ways of expressing the same truths. In Lurianic Kabbalism Adam Kadmon is the first production after the tzimtzum (contraction) within Eyn Sof, and the Sefirot are his emanations.

4 Sometimes it is Being which is said to have the two aspects which correspond to those we have just mentioned. On this cf. Fakhruddin 'Iraqi: Divine Flashes, tr. by W. C. Chittick and P. L. Wilson (New York: Paulist Press, 1982), pp. 6-17.

5 Here we can see a connection with Manu who is the Lord for a particular cycle.

6 On the level of Universal Manifestation the first production is the Universal (or Divine) Spirit from whence proceeds the Universal Soul (the subtle realm which is properly thought of as demiurgic) and, in turn, the physical world (the World Body). We should point out that some writers, in discussing the stages of creation, use the term "Being" where we use the term "Existence." For an example of this cf. Toshihiko Izutsu, A Comparative Study of the Key Concepts in Sufism and Taoism (Tokyo: Keio Institute of Cultural and Linguistic Studies, 1966), p. 118.

7 We have used the words "creation" and "manifestation" interchangeably, but it must be noted that the two have somewhat different connotations. The esoteric term "manifestation" does not imply separateness from God, whereas the exoteric or religious term "creation" does carry this implication. In the one case we say that God (as Being) manifests Himself as the world, and in the other case that God creates the world. The first implies that the world has no reality apart from God.

8 In connection with the stages of creation ending with the polarization of Being we must call the reader's attention to the first two lines of Chapter 42 of the Tao Te Ching: "The Tao bore the One and the One bore the Two." The One corresponds to Being (referred to as "The Uncarved Block" in Chapters 19, 28, 32, and 37) and the Two--Heaven (T'ien) and Earth (T'i)--

correspond to Purusha and Prakriti. The phrase "Mother Earth" refers even more profoundly to the Earth as a symbol of Prakriti. Te (virtue, uprightness, or power) in the Tao Te Ching, which is what all things possess of the Tao and by virtue of which they exist and are what they are, seems to correspond to what we have called the Divine influence, although it may also be called the influence of Heaven.

9 Alternatively, we could understand Anaximander's apeiron as the equivalent of the Hindu akasa (ether, quinta essentia), the fifth element from which are derived fire, earth, air, and water. However, the first interpretation seems preferable. Whether Anaximander's apeiron theory was really given in opposition to Thales' postulation of water as the origin and substratum of all things depends of whether Thales was talking about physical water or only using water in the traditional way as a metaphor for the passive pole of creation. Even if he was talking about physical water we should keep in mind that he meant it as the substance of the whole cosmos, and not just the physical world.

10 While we cannot quite identify the Logos with Being we can say that it issues from the heart of Being. Of course, we are speaking here of the Biblical Logos, not the Logos of Heraclitus or the Alexandrian Logos of Philo, Clement and Origen.

11 The Universal Intellect or Spirit, also called the Solar Ray, the World Spirit, the Heavenly Ray, the Golden Thread, and the Divine Ray or Spirit. (It should be noted that Guénon uses the phrase "Universal Spirit" to refer to the Presence of the Unmanifest in the universe, and thus as the equivalent of the Shekhinah in Judaism.) From the human perspective the Divine establishes its Presence in the individual through the medium of the Celestial Ray which connects all beings with each other and with the Spiritual Sun (Being), and hence with the Unmanifest Itself. We have not mentioned the Holy Spirit of Judaism and Christianity in this context because the correlations appear to be different. Apart from Its later adoption as one of the Persons of the Trinity the Holy Spirit is found to correspond either to the Presence of God or to the Divine influence. That is to say, the phrase "Holy Spirit" has been used to denote both things, and thus we are faced with something which seems to fall between the usual categories. The same is true of Te in Taoism (cf. footnote 8) and there may be in this a point of correspondence between the traditions of East and West.

12 "Berahah" in Hebrew and "barakah" in Arabic.

13 Aperçus sur l'Initiation (Paris: Éditions Traditionnelles, 1980), Chapter IV.

14 On the comparison between individual regeneration and cosmic generation cf. Philo's Questions and Answers on Exodus, Book I, Section 23.

15 This story indicates particularly the sacrificial character of creation.

16 In Kabbalism Hokhmah projects the Third Sefira Binah which is called the Mother of the other Sefirot and the rest of creation. This is quite comparable to the Hindu Maya, worshipped as the Mother, which can be taken as equivalent to Prakriti (cf. Chapter 12, footnote 11). Similarly, Plato, in the Timaeus (49-50), describes the passive pole as the receptacle, the nurse of all generation, that in which generation takes place, and the natural recipient of all impressions. It bears mentioning that the word "Prakriti" should not, as is often done, be translated by the word "Nature." It is not so much that such a translation is completely wrong as that it may be misleading. Today, most people understand the term "nature" to mean the physical world, but Prakriti is not merely the "mother" of the physical world, but of the psychic and spiritual as well.

17 There seems to be an allusion to this process in Hymn X, 129 of the Rig Veda where we start out with the One who breathed windless and who by tapas (austerity, heat) produced the world. An interesting Mordvinian variant of these stories which employs the symbolism of friends is mentioned by Mircea Eliade:

> God was alone on a rock. "If only I had a brother, I would make the World!" he said, and he spat on the Waters. From his spittle a mountain was born. God split it with his sword, and out of the mountain came the Devil (Satan). As soon as he appeared the Devil proposed to God that they should be brothers and create the World together. "We will not be brothers, but companions," answered God. And together they proceeded to the creation of the World.

[The Two and the One, tr. by J. M. Cohen (New York: Harper & Row, 1965), pp. 85-86.] Eliade relates that in other stories the creators of the world are understood as brothers (Ibid. pp. 82-85). This is not the place to discuss the idea of God and the devil as friends or brothers. We must remember that folk tales present a somewhat impure or corrupt form of traditional wisdom. For instance, the waters that the brothers or friends walk on before creation cannot be assimilated to Prakriti in the main sense of the term. However, they might refer to the sea of infinite possibilities contained in the Unmanifest. Eliade also mentions a Bulgarian legend according to which God and His shadow combine to create the world (Ibid. p. 86), and we find a similar story told about the Egyptian god Ra and his shadow.

18
There are stories in which a being symbolizing the active pole slays another being symbolizing the passive pole in order to bring about creation. A well-known Hindu example involves the slaying of the serpent Vritra by Indra, of which the story of St. George and the dragon is a distant echo. Serpents and serpentine creatures like the dragon are used as symbols of the substance of the cosmos for two reasons. They resemble both rope with its coils and twists and the sea with its waves. Rope is a symbol of the passive pole of Existence in that it is ordinarily made up of separate strands, just as the stuff of the cosmos is generally conceived as a mixture, though one which is completely homogenized. (At least it is conceived as a mixture of tendencies, viz., the three gunas.) The sea is such a symbol because it consists of the plastic element water and because it surrounds land and thus appears all-encompassing. On the matter of rope, when braided or twisted it becomes a symbol of the cosmos. Many of the torii or entrance gates of Shinto shrines in Japan (namely those in the so-called Churen style, which may well be the oldest) consist of two wooden poles with a braided rope stretched between them on which five tufts of rope hang. The gates would seem to symbolize the cosmos stretched between the active and passive poles of creation. The tufts would stand for the five basic elements (cf. footnote 9). The braiding of the rope would also symbolize the constant flow or change in the cosmos. Of special interest is the extremely thick sacred rope hung in front of the worship hall of the Grand Shrine of Izumo. It is coiled rather than braided, and three tufts of rope (rather than the usual five) hang from it. This may be mere coincidence, but the three tufts could symbolize the three worlds. The rope, since it is only coiled and not braided may be an intermediate symbol and thus stand for the substance of the world as well. In that case the tufts would stand for the three tendencies

111

which inhere in it. The Shinto conception of Nature (in the broad sense of the term—cf. footnote 16) as holy is comparable, on a certain level, to the Hindu worship of Maya.

[19] This phrase can also be used as a description of the Divine Spirit since the Spirit is the locus of the Activity of Heaven (cf. Chapter 12).

[20] Guénon has pointed out that we can find symbols of Heaven and Earth in Masonry. This pair of principles is symbolized by the plumb-line and level, the compass and try-square, and the try-square itself considered in a different way. Cf. _La Grande Triade_ (Paris: Gallimard, 1957), pp. 34, 128, and 133.

[21] Philo, _On the Creation_, tr. by G. H. Whitaker (Cambridge: Harvard University Press, 1929), Section XXXIII.

[22] _Ibid._, Section XXXIII.

[23] For more on the symbolism of the first six days cf. René Guénon's _Symbolism of the Cross_, Chapter IV.

Chapter 11

In the Image of God

> And God created man in His image, in
> the image of God He created him; male
> and female He created them.
> (<u>Genesis</u>, Chapter 1, Verse 27)

The ancient Greek philosopher Xenophanes once wrote:

> The Ethiopians say that their gods
> are snub-nosed and black, the
> Thracians that theirs have light blue
> eyes and red hair. But if cattle and
> horses or lions had hands, or were
> able to draw with their hands and do
> the works that men can do, horses
> would draw the forms of the gods like
> horses, and cattle like cattle, and
> they would make their bodies such as
> they each had themselves.[1]

It is unfortunate that even today in our "enlightened civilization" many people still do take literally the idea that we are made in God's image. The picture of God as an old man residing in the heavens has not yet disappeared from our consciousness. But it must be admitted that most people have outgrown this view, a leftover from childish religion. What then is the meaning of this "in His image"? It is a truism that simple questions have complicated answers, and this case is no exception to the rule. In fact, it is an instance of the rule <u>par</u> <u>excellence</u>.

What complicates matters is that there are really two images of God. In the lesser sense we can say that the manifested world is such an image, while in the higher sense it is Being which is an image of God. Put differently we could say that both the mundane and archetypal worlds are images, although the former is really an image of the image. What further compounds our problems is that it is Edenic or Primordial Man who is said to be made in the image of God, and thus the typical human of our times cannot claim this distinction, except as a potentiality.

Taking the lesser sense of "image" first, we may recall that the atomist Democritus of ancient Greece called man a microcosm (or little world system) in contrast to the macrocosm (the great world system or

cosmos).[2]   In   his   excellent   book,   An Introduction to
Sufi Doctrine, Titus Burckhardt, extending the thought
of   Pascal,   remarks,   ". . . the world or the macrocosm
clearly 'contains' man who is himself   its   integrating
part.   But man knows the world and, given the principial unity of Being and Knowledge, this means   that   all
possibilities   of   the world are in a virtual and principial sense present in man." He adds, ". . . man is a
qualitative 'abridgement' of the great   cosmic   'book,'
all   universal   qualities   being   in one way or another
expressed in his form."   And   he   quotes   St. Gregory
Palamas   as   saying, "Man, this greater world in little
compass, is an epitome of all that exists   in   a   unity
and is the crown of Divine works."[3]

It   is obvious that a human being combines aspects
of the mineral, vegetable, and   animal   kingdoms.   As
well   he partakes of the physical, subtle, and formless
realms, although he may not be aware of the latter two.
And while the Divine Spirit or Intellect   pervades   all
of   creation, it is present within man in a special way
which enables him to grasp his true relationship to God
and achieve the sense of eternity.   It is perhaps   with
this   in   mind that Maimonides discusses the meaning of
man's being created in God's image in   the   very   first
chapter   of   The Guide of the Perplexed.   At the end of
that chapter we find the following statement:

> Now   man   possesses   as   his proprium
> something in him that is very strange
> as it is not found in   anything   else
> that   exists   under the sphere of the
> moon, namely, intellectual   apprehen-
> sion.   In   the exercise of this, no
> sense, no part of the body,   none   of
> the   extremities are used; and there-
> fore this apprehension was   likened
> unto   the   apprehension of the deity,
> which does not require an instrument,
> although in reality it   is   not   like
> the   latter   apprehension,   but   only
> appears so to the first strivings   of
> opinion.   It   was   because   of this
> something, I mean because of the   di-
> vine   intellect   conjoined   with man,
> that it is said of the latter that he
> is in the image of God and in His
> likeness,   not   that   God,   may He be
> exalted, is a body   and   possesses   a
> shape.

Although this quotation takes us away from our comparison   of   microcosm   to macrocosm it serves to point out

that besides containing something of what everything else in the universe has, man possesses as well something which no other being has, namely the capability of intellectual apprehension, and thus expresses the cosmos in the most complete way. In the face of the modern mentality we must stress that the intellect is not to be confused with mere reason which may deal with generalizations about individual things. Rather, the intellect is what enables us to grasp the supra-individual or universal. It is the presence of the intellect which gives us the potential for spiritual perfection.

Turning to the higher sense of "image" it is Being or the Archetypal World, the first revelation of God, which will concern us. Being is explicitly pictured as the Cosmic Person in both Hinduism, as Purusha, and Kabbalism, as Adam Kadmon. It is perhaps in Kabbalism that we have the clearest indication of what the phrase "image of God" means, for the Sefirot serve as an integrated picture of the possibilities inherent in God which are actualized in creation. As to the other side of the comparison, it is Edenic or Primordial Man—Adam—who, as a perfect picture of the original Unity of Existence, can be thought of as made in the image of the Oneness of Being.

In order to understand the nature of Edenic Man we will have to focus on the phrase "male and female He created them" (Genesis, Chapter 1, Verse 27). This is a clear reference to androgynous man, and we must recall in this connection the story of the creation of the human race in Plato's Symposium (189D and E) where the original androgyne splits into male and female and thence propagates the human race. We find confirmation of the androgynous nature of Adam in Verses 21-22 of Chapter 2 when Eve is produced from Adam's rib. Androgynous man may also be considered as the complete man, balancing in himself the masculine and feminine aspects of Existence and integrating in himself all of the elements of our particular state of existence. This is true by virtue of Adam's place in the Terrestrial Paradise, the center point of the manifestation of our state of existence which in a sense contains all things within it. Al-Arabi goes even further than this in describing Adam as the Perfect Man:

> He has expressed this polarity of qualities [in the Qur'an] as being His Hands devoted to the creation of the Perfect Man who integrates in himself all Cosmic realities and their individual [manifesta- tions]. . . . he [man] unites [in

himself] the two modes, the [originated] Cosmos and the [originating and original] Reality, which are His two hands.[4]

In this way Adam integrates within himself all of the levels of manifestation and can be considered God's "Vice-Regent."[5] Thus Adam is King of the World, and since God is considered the Ultimate King (or King of kings), we can see still another meaning of the phrase "in His image." Adam's role as King is shown in Chapter 1, Verse 28 of Genesis: "God blessed them [the androgyne Adam-Eve] and said to them, 'Be fertile and increase, fill the earth and master it; rule the fish of the sea, the birds of the sky, and all the living things that creep on earth.'" Somewhat related to this is a further meaning of "in His image" which is brought out in Verse 20 of Chapter 2 when Adam, before the split into Adam and Eve, names all the animals. On the Divine level naming is tantamount to creating—"In the beginning was the Word" (John, Chapter 1, Verse 1)—and Adam's naming the animals is really a reflection of the Divine activity.

For Al-Arabi, Adam is what is often called in esotericism the Universal Man, and as such is the perfect image of the original Universal Man—Being. However, in order to avoid confusion it is best to use the term "Perfect Man" or "Transcendent Man" for Adam. Such a being, though the product of Heaven and Earth, through realizing his essential identity with God has been liberated from the cosmos. He resides not only at the center of our state of being, but of all states of being and thus is virtually identical to the Divine Ray which connects all the states of being to their source. It is in this regard that he is symbolized by the cross[6] and may be identified as the Way to God. Piercing through the center of the Divine Sun or Being (and thereby united with the Unmanifest beyond Being) he can even be considered as the Logos or Divine Word. And this can be more easily understood if we remember that viewed as the Divine Spirit he separates Heaven and Earth, which allows creation to occur, and at the same time unites Heaven and Earth so that creation actually takes place. With these thoughts in mind we can more easily understand the following statement of Al-Arabi:

> For the Reality, he is as the pupil is for the eye through which the act of seeing takes place. Thus he is called insan [meaning both man and pupil], for it is by him that the Reality looks on His creation and be-

116

stows the Mercy [of existence] on them. He is Man, the transient [in his form], the eternal [in his essence]; he is the perpetual, the everlasting, the [at once] discriminating and unifying Word. It is by his existence that the Cosmos subsists and he is, in relation to the Cosmos, as the seal is to the ring, the seal being that place whereon is engraved the token with which the king seals his treasure. So he is called the Vice-Regent, for by him God preserves His creation, as the seal preserves the king's treasure. So long as the king's seal is on it no one dares to open it except by his permission,' the seal being [as it were] a regent in charge of the kingdom. Even so is the Cosmos preserved so long as the Perfect Man remains in it.[7]

Following the comments in Chapter 2, it is best to view the figure of Adam in the Biblical account of creation as the Prototype of man, rather than a human being. However, as such he represents what is possible for human beings, and any human who has realized his identity with the Unmanifest--that is to say, any Perfect Man--is for all intents and purposes identical with the original Adam.

Guénon, in various works, steadfastly refuses to identify Adam with the Perfect Man. Rather, he views Adam as the True Man who resides at the center of our state of being but not all the other states. The True Man is one who has reached the end of the path initiated by the first rebirth but not as yet that of the second rebirth and thus has not realized the Supreme Identity. We can perhaps reconcile these two descriptions of Adam by saying that on one level he represents the Prototype of man and on another level (or from a different point of view) he represents human beings of the Edenic or Golden Age. The normal man of that age was already centered in the Divine Spirit and only had to undergo what we have called liberation from the human state. If Adam is viewed in this way then we must say that the typical human of today is made in an image of the image of God. If Adam is viewed in the first way, then we must consider ourselves as made in the image twice removed.

[1] G. S. Kirk, J. E. Raven and M. Schofield, The Presocratic Philosophers, Second Edition (Cambridge University Press, 1983), Fragments 168-169.

[2] In Sufism the macrocosm is called al-insan al kabir (the Great Man), and Plato, in the Timaeus (30C and D), refers to it as "a Living Creature." Similar to the view of Democritus is Philo's notion of the cosmos as a great plant and man as a small, though special, plant within it. This is found in his book Concerning Noah's Work as a Planter, Sections I to IV. In ancient times the macrocosm was considered by others to be God Himself. But this pantheistic view, besides being incorrect, does away with the notion of the cosmos as image of God.

[3] Titus Burckhardt, An Introduction to Sufi Doctrine, tr. by D. M. Matheson (Lahore: Sh. Muhammad Ashraf, 1959), pp. 88-89.

[4] Ibn Al' Arabi: The Bezels of Wisdom, tr. by R. W. J. Austin (New York: Paulist Press, 1980), pp. 55 and 56.

[5] Ibid., p. 51.

[6] The horizontal bar indicates our particular state of existence, with the others, which we may term the heavens and hells, above and below that line.

[7] Ibid., p. 51.

Chapter 12

Adam and Eve

Perhaps the most well-known story in the Torah is that of the fall of Adam and Eve in the Garden of Eden. But as much as it is known, so much is it misunderstood. There have been no lack of interpretations of this story, and many of them have been symbolic. But because the people making these interpretations have approached the story in such wrong-headed ways, the results, as we might expect, have been less than edifying.

According to the literalistic view, every sentence in the story is to be taken historically and considered true. In opposition to this is the scientistic view: every sentence is to be taken historically and considered false. Some of this group, in an attempt to be charitable, find in the story of the fall the first recorded example of the theory of evolution: from the innocent ape to man.

Then we have the moralistic interpretation. According to this view, the story of the fall (like the rest of the stories in the Bible) is not literally true but serves as a backdrop for teaching certain moral lessons.

The structuralistic idea is that the story is not literally true but demonstrates the essentially binary nature of human thought. For example, the passage from naked to clothed represents the civilizing force of society exerted on life as it would be in a state of nature. According to another anthropological view the leaving of paradise symbolizes the passage from a gathering culture to a farming culture. Finally, the psychologistic views. According to one of these the expulsion from the Garden symbolizes birth and its attendant trauma. According to another the loss of innocence and subsequent expulsion from the Garden represents growing up (reaching puberty) and leaving home. About these last two views it must be said that the birth trauma is a modern invention and that in Biblical times people lived for the most part in extended family units.

None of these approaches takes seriously the possibility that the creators of this and other stories to be found in the Bible were consciously attempting to transmit spiritual truths in a symbolic fashion. Some atheists view these stories as folk tales and conclude that they are of entertainment value at best. This approach is half correct and half incorrect. These stories are at least akin to folk tales, but the proper conclusion to draw from this is that they have great significance on a symbolic level.[1]

As we have already admitted, most Bible stories function on different levels, and the story of the fall is no exception to this rule. On the most superficial level it explains how snakes lost their legs and became enemies of mankind. On a somewhat more profound level it explains why life has to be so hard and why people have to die.[2] Of course, the explanation for our hard lot which is offered in Genesis is not satisfactory to many people. If someone who had never heard of Judaism or Christianity read the account of the disobedience and punishment of Adam and Eve described in Chapter 3, he might well come away with a very negative opinion of God. On a literal level the whole episode reads like the story of a parent who told his children not to eat the fruit of a certain tree on his property and who punished their disobedience by running them out of his house and sentencing them to hard labor followed by execution. For all the fuss that is made over the Biblical disobedience by literalists (most of whom do not understand the true meaning of "obedience to God") it is hard to see the story as reflecting positively on God. But it is precisely this bad taste left in our mouths that should alert us to the possibility that we are not approaching the story in the proper manner. If someone who had never heard of citrus fruits was given an orange with the information that it was a fruit, he might just bite right into it. The rind would taste quite bitter and he might conclude that this was one fruit which was not worth eating. But if he was then given a little more information about the orange he would most likely eat it properly and reverse his judgment. The literal meaning of the story of the fall is just its outside, and is not very palatable. But like the orange, it has an inside, a symbolic meaning which is full of spiritual nourishment.

Before getting to the "inside" of the story we must clear up a humorous misunderstanding which has arisen in the minds of some people due to the connection between sexual awareness and death in the story of the fall. These people have drawn the conclusion that the way to long life is abstention from sexual activity. While sexual awareness is certainly a problem for the spiritual life, and while over-indulgence in any way can lead to an early death, the view we are considering cannot be taken seriously. For the general well-being and stability of life on this planet it is imperative that animals which reproduce sexually be subject to death.

In order to begin a serious consideration of the story of the fall we must put aside completely the idea that it recounts an historical event. Its value lies in its being true for all times and persons, and it is in this respect that we all suffer the effects of "original sin." However, while it does not recount an historical event, we may say that it symbolizes one-- the fall of humanity during the Golden Age--and in this regard as well we can say that we all suffer its effects. Indeed, because of the central position of man in the cosmos (which we touched upon in the last chapter) the fall_3 of mankind involved the fall of the whole of creation.³

The fall is prefigured in the splitting of the androgynous Adam into Adam and Eve. On the universal level it symbolizes the splitting of Purusha and Prakriti which necessarily precedes creation. And just as the splitting of Adam necessarily results in the imperfection of Adam and Eve which leads to their fall, the splitting of the Unity of Existence into the duality of Purusha and Prakriti (Heaven and Earth, the wind and the waters) necessarily results in the imperfection of the cosmos which leads to its fall. This imperfection of the cosmos is often referred to as the evil in the world, and it is hardly necessary to mention that much ink has been used in trying to account for its existence.

As Spinoza pointed out, much of what we call evil is merely what we do not happen to like. Thus we dignify as absolute something that is quite relative. However, this sort of self-centered attitude goes to the central nature of evil: it is the predation of one thing on another. If there was no multiplicity but only a unity then there could be no evil. But if there was no multiplicity, if there was no separation of the poles of Existence, then there would be no cosmos. That there are even two things implies the possibility of what we call evil. Viewing this same subject from a somewhat higher perspective we may cite two very succinct comments by Frithjof Schuon:

> What people fail to understand is
> that the divine nature implies mani-
> festation, creation, objectivation,
> and what is "other-than-the-Self,"
> and that this projection implies im-
> perfection and therefore evil, since
> what is "other-than-God" cannot be

121

> perfect, God alone being good. . . .
> The whole problem lies in that fact
> that the serpent was in Paradise.
> Had he not been there Paradise would
> have been God, or rather it could not
> have had any separate existence. To
> exist means not to be God, and so to
> be "evil."[4]

In connection with the first comment we should recall
the statement of Jesus, "No one is good but God alone"
(Mark, Chapter 10, Verse 18). It is best to use the
word "perfect" in preference to "good" when one is
describing God, for using the latter term gives the im-
pression that we are judging God in moral terms, and He
is quite beyond such categories which can only have to
do with the multiplicity of Universal Existence.

Returning to the subject of the splitting of the
androgynous Adam we can say that it results in two
incomplete halves. Now this is, of course, the current
human position, and it is of interest to examine the
various human responses to this loss of completeness,
or as we might describe it, this loss of the balance
between the active and passive poles of creation as
objectified in us. One response is engaging in sexual
intercourse. The problem here is that besides the fact
that only the physical side of the person is involved,
the effect of unification lasts a very short time. A
much higher response is marriage which engages the emotional and mental sides of the person (and in general
the soul) and is or should be a long-term matter. A
much lower response is the orgy, although it has
evidently not always been so viewed.

Here we must pause for a moment to correct a mis-
conception found in the writing of Eliade and others
having to do with the aim of recapturing the primordial
completeness or unity.[5] According to these commentators what people are aiming at in rituals designed to
bring about such a unity is an experiential return to
the primordial burbling soup, the original chaos in
which all opposites are united. It may be that in certain degenerate societies this parody of a spiritual
idea has provided a justification of orgiastic rituals.
According to this way of thinking our great aim is to
bring about a state of chaos internally and externally
as a way of cancelling out internal and external division. It is said that the demonic apes the Divine, and
this is a case in point, but we must never mistake this
distortion of spirituality for the real thing.

In the first place the aim of regaining the androgynous state has to do not with a reunion of opposites but with a uniting of complements—the masculine and feminine poles of creation. The resultant condition is very far from chaos, the latter being the natural state of one of the two poles. In the second place, achieving the androgynous state is a spiritual rather than a physical matter and thus cannot be brought about by physical or external activities. Obviously the sexual act can be taken as a symbol of the rejoining of the two poles of creation and thus invested with more than a physical significance. Indeed, in the Upanishads it is given a sacrificial significance, and it can very easily be understood as symbolizing the creative activity of the masculine pole acting on the feminine pole. But none of this implies that the act can bring about spiritual regeneration.[6] Again we must say that the reintegration of the person is a spiritual one, and it is to this that the passages from the Gospel According to Thomas mentioned by Eliade refer. In Logion 22 we read:

> Jesus said to them: When you make the two one, and when you make the inner as the outer and the outer as the inner and the above as the below, and when you make the male and the female into a single one, so that the male will not be male and the female (not) be female . . then you shall enter [the Kingdom].[7]

And in Logion 106 we read:

> Jesus said: When you make the two one, you shall become sons of Man, and when you say: "Mountain be moved," it will be moved.[8]

These quotations, which would otherwise be puzzling, take on an obvious significance in light of our discussion. In order to enter the Kingdom of God, in order to become sons of Man (the androgynous Adam) we must reverse the process of the original splitting into Adam and Eve and become whole again. This reversal can be described as regaining Paradise or as regaining the fruits of the Tree of Life.

The Terrestrial Paradise has been called by many names: the Garden of Eden, the Land of the Hyperboreans, the Isle of the Blessed, and Ultima Thule among others. In many cultures there are stories of

123

such lands, pictured sometimes atop inaccessible mountains, sometimes on far away islands, and sometimes atop mountains on islands. Unfortunately, these lands, which survive all floods, have become invisible in our times. They are symbols of the center of Divine influence on earth, and their indestructability despite all the cataclysms and the degeneration of the world symbolizes the persistence of this influence. Their invisibility in our age symbolizes the spiritual blindness which is obvious throughout the world.[9] While we must understand these paradisiacal lands in a symbolic way we can admit that at all times there have existed spiritual centers which can be regarded as the focal points of spiritual influence in the world.

Philo also rejects the idea of an external Paradise and locates it along with the Tree of Life and the Tree of Knowledge of Good and Evil within the soul.[10] There is little doubt that these trees do exist within us, but we must also note that the Tree of Life is to be understood first and foremost as the World Axis--the Divine Spirit around which our realm and all others are manifested. In Taoism it is called the Middle Way (as the center of the various realms of existence) and the Way of Heaven (since it is the path of the Influence or Will of Heaven). We have noted that it is sometimes symbolized by fire and we can add that it is also pictured as a mountain and as rising smoke. It is along this Axis that we find the Divine Presence in the world.[11]

The central position of the Tree of Life is shown by the four rivers which begin in Garden of Eden and flow out into the rest of the world (Genesis, Chapter 2, Verse 10). These rivers symbolize the four directions of space and we can view them as dividing the earth into four quarters radiating out from the center of manifestation. It is worth noticing that the Land of the Garden is not watered from above "but a flow would well up from the ground and water the whole surface of the earth" (Chapter 2, Verse 6). Generally, God's inspiration, influence, and sustenance are thought of as coming from on high. As rain, which is sustaining and purifying, also comes from on high it is a natural symbol for God's influence. However, in the Garden of Eden there is no rain but rather a flow of water from the ground. This flow also symbolizes God's influence, and as it comes from the ground rather than from on high we can conclude that in some sense the Garden and the trees within it are in the midst of God. That is to say, when we are positioned at the Tree of Life in the midst of the Garden, God is not "up there" but "right here."

Just as we can speak of the center of the world as a whole we can also speak of the center of the human being. We are all connected to the Divine Spirit by our own spirits, and we can re-express this by saying that the Divine Spirit runs through all of us. Thus the Terrestrial Paradise and the Tree of Life can be seen as existing within each human being. Indeed, as far as spiritual growth is concerned it is necessary to think of them as within, and understand the journey to them as an inner one. Androgynous Adam, the Perfect Man, resides in consciousness at the center of his being. There he experiences completeness and unity with all the other beings of the earth. This is shown in Verses 29-30 of Chapter 1 where God gives the fruits and seeds of plants to man as food. One who discerns his unity with the rest of creation does not want to harm any living thing as a means of feeding himself.

The experience of unity is shattered when Adam and Eve eat of the Tree of Knowledge of Good and Evil, and the change which comes over them is really the fall into dualistic consciousness. Once one experiences the world in terms of oneself and others, mine and thine, good and bad, the fall has occurred. It is not accidental that sexual awareness is linked with the fall, for it is at the time of puberty that humans lose the last vestige of the primordial world-view. Before it they had been complete (not needing a sexual partner) and balanced (containing male and female aspects in nearly equal amounts). Internally they were neuter and externally they treated others in this way. But with the dawning of sexual awareness they begin to see people first and foremost as males and females who are to be treated differently and viewed as objects for the fulfillment of their desires. To sum up, puberty and the coming of sexual awareness is an example on a certain level of the division of androgynous man.

The serpent who tempts Adam and Eve to eat the fatal fruit is, as we indicated in Chapter 1, a dual symbol. The connection between the snake and the tree (or suitable substitute) in spiritual symbols is quite well known. One need think only of the Western caduceus and the archetypal Hindu picture of the Devas and Asuras churning the ocean for its hidden treasure of amrita by pulling on either end of a serpent wrapped around the world mountain. In the first place, the snake, like the Tree of Life itself, is a symbol of immortality. We must remember that the Tree, as the symbol of the Divine Spirit, represents the center of the world as well as every human being. As such, it is the place of immortality or consciousness of the eternal.[12] Adam and Eve's portrayal as immortal before the fall symbolizes the state of consciousness of the complete person. Now the snake is also a symbol of death and rebirth. For this reason it is connected with the Tree of Knowledge since it has both a positive (rebirth) and negative (death) aspect, or as we would put it in moralistic terms, a good and evil aspect. However, on the whole, the snake viewed in this way represents immortality and thus is good in a sense of the term higher than the moralistic one.

The snake as tempter and cause of the fall is a symbol of the world manifested around the Divine Spirit. (Its various coils can be seen as symbolizing either past and future cycles of manifestation or higher and lower states of existence.) The world, through its effects on the senses, draws us ever out and away from the center of our being. Just as a snake entraps a victim by coiling around it the world can be said to entrap us by envelopment. In leading us away from our center it causes us to feel incomplete and thus puts desire in the place of peace. Actually, desire is but one side of a coin whose other side is aversion, and together they lead us to divide the world into what is good and what is evil. The cherubim which God sets to guard the entrance of the Garden of Eden after He has exiled Adam and Eve can be seen as symbolizing this judgmental view of the world.

There is still another way of understanding the fall which is perfectly consistent with the first. As a distancing from the Spirit it represents the development of the psycho-physical individuality and hence the ego. This development involves a sense of separateness from the rest of creation, and subsequently there arises a desire for certain things and an aversion to other things. As before, this leads to evaluation or seeing things as good and evil. The end result is a loss of joy or bliss and the beginning of suffering due to either not getting (or losing) what we desire or getting what we have an aversion to. In our lives, as we mature, it is our fate to be thus cast out of paradise. Our purpose in life is to consciously work to reverse this process. On this subject Frithjof Schuon writes:

> Man complains of his sufferings, such as separation and death; but has he not inflicted them a priori upon the Self, by his very egoity? Is not individuation a separation from the divine "I" and is not the ego itself a death in respect of infinite Life? It will be objected that we are not

responsible for our existence; but man ceaselessly recreates, in his actions, this responsibility which he thinks he does not have; in this, taken together with the foregoing considerations, lies the deeper meaning of original sin. Man suffers because he wishes to be "self" in opposition to "Self". . . .[13]

The Buddhist wheel of existence is comparable as a symbol to a section or cut of the tree surrounded by the snake. In the wheel we observe a place of central repose or peace surrounded by the moving spokes and rim. Typically we find ourselves on the rim of that wheel as it spins around. Our proper goal is to slide down one of the spokes toward the center and thus reach a point where we have stopped spinning--the Terrestrial Paradise. Now we must envision an axle going through this wheel and joining it to another wheel through which it also passes. This axle is the World Axis, and our goal after reaching the Terrestrial Paradise should be to move up this axis through the Celestial Paradise at the "top" of the cosmos, finally achieving what is often called union with God, but which is actually the realization of our already existing identity with God. This journey is an inner one, taking place in the consciousness of the human being. As we said earlier it involves two rebirths, the first of which, as Guénon points out, leads to a return to normalcy, a thing lacking in the life of modern man. The second results in the development of what in the West is called saintliness.

Notes for Chapter 12

1 For more on this matter cf. Ananda Coomaraswamy's excellent article "Primitive Mentality" in Coomaraswamy: Selected Papers, Volume 1 (Princeton: Princeton University Press, 1977), pp. 286-307.

2 There are stories all over the world which explain how mankind had a chance for an easy life or immortality and how some progenitor or culture hero let it slip away either by doing something forbidden or foolish, or by lack of care, or by not being in the right place at the right time, or by being asleep at the important moment. All of these tales have an air about them of lessons for children who are evidently supposed to draw the proper moral. That is not to say that none of them has a deeper meaning.

3 W. L. Wilmshurst, in his book, The Meaning of Masonry (New York: Crown, 1980), takes a similar viewpoint in explaining the symbolism of this story. He goes on to compare the fall of Adam and Eve to the "fall" of Persephone which was the subject of the Eleusinian Mysteries (pp. 193-194).

4 Frithjof Schuon, Spiritual Perspectives and Human Facts, tr. by Macleod Matheson (London: Faber and Faber, 1954), pp. 50 and 52.

5 Cf. Mircea Eliade, The Two and the One, Part II, especially pp. 111-124.

6 If Tantric Buddhism and Hinduism seem like exceptions to this rule it is because they are very poorly understood in the West. For a proper perspective on this matter cf. Marco Pallis, "Considerations on the Tantric Alchemy" in A Buddhist Spectrum (New York: Seabury Press, 1981), Chapter 5, and René Guénon, "Le cinquieme Veda" in Études sur l'Hindouisme (Paris: Éditions Traditionnelles, 1979).

7 A. Guillaumont et al., The Gospel According to Thomas (New York: Harper & Row, 1959), p. 17.

8 Ibid., p. 53.

9 "The word of the Lord came to me: O mortal, you dwell among the rebellious breed. They have eyes to see but see not, ears to hear but hear not; for they are a rebellious breed" (Ezekiel, Chapter 12, Verses 1 and 2).

[10] Cf. Concerning Noah's Work as a Planter, Part IX.

[11] Ultimately we must say that the Divine Presence pervades the world since the world is but a manifestation of God Who contains it. But from our point of view the Presence exists in a central place. The Hindu worship of Maya affirms the absolute point of view. Maya can be equated with the world or cosmos. But it can also be equated with Prakriti, as the latter is the source of the world. Maya is often described as Illusion in that it hides the true character of its underlying Reality--Saguna Brahman or Being. Being is One, but through ignorance we experience it as a plurality of entities in a state of becoming--i.e., as Maya. Thus Maya appears as the manifested world over and against Saguna Brahman. In truth it is but the Shakti or Power (constituting a Veil of Ignorance) of Saguna Brahman and as such is inseparable from It and worthy of worship.

[12] There is no better symbol of the place of immortality than the evergreen tree which is to be found in all Shinto shrines. Shinto priests conducting ceremonies outside of shrines bring along at least one branch of such a tree.

[13] Frithjof Schuon, Gnosis: Divine Wisdom (London: John Murray, 1959), p. 84.

Bibliography

Al-Ghazzali, Abu Hamid Muhammad. The Niche for Lights. Translated by W. H. T. Gairdner. Lahore: Sh. Muhammad Ashraf, 1968.

_____. The Mysteries of Fasting. Translated by N. A. Faris. Lahore: Sh. Muhammad Ashraf, 1968.

Al-Hujwiri, Ali B. Uthman Al-Jullabi. The Kashf Al-Mahjub. Translated by Reynold A. Nicholson. London: Luzac & Company, 1976.

Anshen, Ruth Nanda. The Reality of the Devil: Evil In Man. New York: Dell Publishing Company, 1972.

Aristotle. Metaphysics. Translated by Richard Hope. Ann Arbor: University of Michigan Press, 1963.

Augustine, Saint. Confessions. Translated by R. S. Pine-Coffin. Baltimore: Penguin Books, 1961.

Austin, R. W. J., trans. Ibn Al'Arabi: The Bezels of Wisdom. New York: Paulist Press, 1980.

Batto, Bernard F. "Red Sea or Reed Sea." Biblical Archeology Review (July/August 1984):56-63.

_____. "The Reed Sea: Requiescat in Pace." Journal of Biblical Literature (Volume 102):27-35.

Broudy, Harry. Truth and Credibility. New York: Longman, 1981.

Bühler, Georg, trans. The Laws of Manu. New York: Dover Publications, 1969.

Burckhardt, Titus. An Introduction to Sufi Doctrine. Translated by D. M. Matheson. Lahore: Sh. Muhammad Ashraf, 1959.

Chan, Wing-tsit, trans. The Way of Lao Tzu. Indianapolis: Bobbs-Merrill, 1963.

Chittick, W. C. and Wilson, P.L., trans. Fakhruddin 'Iraqi: Divine Flashes. New York: Paulist Press, 1982.

Deutsch, Eliot, trans. The Bhagavad Gita. New York: Holt, Rinehart and Winston, 1968.

Eliade, Mircea. The Two and the One. Translated by J. M. Cohen. New York: Harper & Row, 1965.

Gaster, Theodor H. Myth, Legend and Custom in the Old Testament, Volume 1. New York: Harper & Row, 1975.

Greer, Rowan A., trans. Origen. New York: Paulist Press, 1979.

Guénon, René. Aperçus sur l'ésotérisme chrétion. Paris: Galli-mard, 1954.

_____. Aperçus sur l'Initiation. Paris: Éditions Tradition-nelles, 1980.

_____. Études sur l'Hindouisme. Paris: Éditions Tradition-nelles, 1979.

_____. Formes Traditionnelles et Cycles Cosmiques. Paris: Gallimard, 1970.

_____. La Grande Triade. Paris: Gallimard, 1957.

_____. Man and His Becoming According to Vedanta. Translated by Charles Whitby. London: Rider & Co., 1929.

_____. The Reign of Quantity. Translated by Lord Northbourne. Baltimore: Penguin Books, 1972.

_____. Le Roi du Monde. Paris: Gallimard, 1958. (Translated under the title The Lord of the World. Ripon, North York-shire: Coombe Springs Press, 1983.)

_____. Symboles fondamentaux de la Science sacrée. Paris: Gallimard, 1962.

_____. Symbolism of the Cross. Translated by Angus McNab. Lon-don: Luzac & Company, 1958.

Guillaumont, A. et al. The Gospel According to Thomas. New York: Harper & Row, 1959.

Halkin, A. S. "Yedaiah Bedershi's Apology." In Jewish Medieval and Renaissance Studies, edited by Alexander Altmann. Cambridge: Harvard University Press, 1967.

Heschel, Abraham Joshua. The Circle of the Baal Shem Tov. Edited by Samuel H. Dresner. Chicago: The University of Chicago Press, 1985.

_____. The Earth is the Lord's and The Sabbath. Cleveland: The World Publishing Company, 1963.

Hesse, Hermann. My Belief. Edited by Theodore Ziolkowski and translated by Denver Lindley. New York: Farrar, Straus and Giroux, 1974.

Hillers, Delbert R. Covenant: History of a Biblical Idea. Baltimore: The Johns Hopkins Press, 1969.

Hügel, Friedrich von. Mystical Elements in Religion, Volume 1. London: Dent & Sons, 1923.

Israel, Manasseh ben. Conciliator. Translated by E. H. Lindo. New York: Hermon Press, 1972.

Izutsu, Toshihiko. A Comparative Study of the Key Concepts in Sufism and Taoism. Tokyo: Keio Institute of Cultural and Linguistic Studies, 1966.

Jacobsen, Thorkeld. The Sumerian King List. Chicago: University of Chicago Press, 1939.

Kalupahana, David J. Buddhist Philosophy: A Historical Analysis. Honolulu: The University Press of Hawaii, 1976.

Kirk, G. S., Raven, J. E. and Schofield, M. The Presocratic Philosophers, Second Edition. Cambridge: Cambridge University Press, 1983.

Lal, P., trans. Dhammapada. New York: Farrar, Straus & Giroux, 1967.

Leach, Edmund. "Nobody Lives in the Real World." Psychology Today (July 1974):61-70.
_____, and Aycock, D. Alan. Structuralist Interpretations of Biblical Myth. New York: Cambridge University Press, 1983.

Lipsey, Roger, ed. Coomaraswamy: Selected Papers, Volume 1. Princeton: Princeton University Press, 1977.

Luk, Charles. Secrets of Chinese Meditation. London: Rider & Co., 1964.

Maimonides, Moses. The Guide of the Perplexed. Translated by Shlomo Pines. Chicago: The University of Chicago Press, 1963.

Malherbe, Abraham J. and Ferguson, Everett, trans. Gregory of Nyssa: The Life of Moses. New York: Paulist Press, 1978.

Meier, Fritz. "The Mystery of the Ka'ba: Symbol and Reality in Islamic Mysticism." In The Mysteries, edited by Joseph Campbell. Princeton: Princeton University Press, 1971.

Middleton, John, ed. Myth and Cosmos. Garden City: The Natural History Press, 1967.

Nasr, Seyyed Hossein. "The Gnostic Tradition." In Science and Civilization in Islam. New York: New American Library, 1968.
_____. "Post-Avicennan Islamic Philosophy and the Study of Being." In Philosophies of Existence, edited by Parviz Morewedge. New York: Fordham University Press, 1982.

Nikhilananda, S., trans. The Gospel of Sri Ramakrishna. New York: Ramakrishna-Vivekananda Center, 1973.

O'Flaherty, Wendy Doniger, trans. The Rig Veda. New York: Penguin Books, 1981.

Origen. On First Principles. Translated by G. W. Butterworth. Gloucester: Peter Smith, 1973.

Orwell, George. Collected Essays, Journalism & Letters, Volumes 1-4. Edited by Sonia Orwell and Ian Angus. New York: Harcourt, Brace, Jovanovich, 1968.

Pallis, Marco. A Buddhist Spectrum. New York: Seabury Press, 1981.

Peters, F. E. Greek Philosophical Terms. New York: New York University Press, 1967.

Philo. Concerning Noah's Works as a Planter. Translated by F. H. Colson and G. H. Whitaker. Cambridge: Harvard University Press, 1968.
_____. On Flight and Finding. Translated by F. H. Colson and G. H. Whitaker. Cambridge: Harvard University Press, 1968.
_____. On the Account of the World's Creation Given by Moses. Translated by F. H. Colson and G. H. Whitaker. Cambridge: Harvard University Press, 1971.
_____. Questions and Answers On Exodus. Translated by Ralph Marcus. Cambridge: Harvard University Press, 1970.
_____. Who is the Heir of Divine Things. Translated by F. H. Colson. Cambridge: Harvard University Press, 1968.

Picker, Stuart D. B. Shinto: Japan's Spiritual Roots. Tokyo: Kodansha International, 1980.

Plato. The Timaeus. In The Dialogues of Plato, Fourth Edition, translated by Benjamin Jowett. Oxford: Oxford University Press, 1953.

Plutarch. "Concerning the Face Which Appears in the Orb of the Moon." Translated by Harold Cherniss and William C. Hembold. In Moralia, Volume XII. Cambridge: Harvard University Press, 1968.
_____. "On the Sign of Socrates." Translated by Phillip H. DeLacy and Benedict Einerson. In Moralia, Volume VII. Cambridge: Harvard University Press, 1968.

Pritchard, James B., ed. Ancient Near Eastern Texts, Third Edition. Princeton: Princeton University Press, 1969.

Radhakrishnan, Sarvepalli. Eastern Religion and Western Thought. New York: Oxford University Press, 1959.
_____, trans. The Principle Upanishads. London: George Allen & Unwin, 1974.

Rumi, Jalaluddin. The Mathnawi. Translated by Reynald A. Nicholson. London: Luzac & Co., 1977.

Schimmel, Annemarie. Mystical Dimension of Islam. Chapel Hill: The University of North Carolina Press, 1975.

Scholem, Gershom. "Kabbalah." In _Encyclopaedia Judaica_, Volume 10. Jerusalem: Keter, 1972.

————. _Major Trends in Jewish Mysticism_. New York: Schocken, 1954.

Schuon, Frithjof. "Alternations In Semitic Monotheism." _Studies in Comparative Religion_ (Summer 1977):166-187.

————. _Esotericism as Principle and as Way_. Translated by William Stoddart. Bedfont, Middlesex: Perennial Books, 1981.

————. _Gnosis: Divine Wisdom_. Translated by G. E. H. Palmer. London: John Murray, 1959.

————. _In the Tracks of Buddhism_. Translated by Marco Pallis. London: George Allen & Unwin, 1968.

————. _Islam and the Perennial Philosophy_. Translated by J. Peter Hobson. World of Islam Festival Publishing Company, 1976.

————. _Logic and Transcendence_. Translated by Peter N. Townsend. New York: Harper & Row, 1975.

————. _Spiritual Perspectives and Human Facts_. Translated by Macleod Matheson. London: Faber and Faber, 1954.

Senzaki, Nyogen and McCandless, Ruth Strout, trans. _The Iron Flute_. Tokyo: Charles E. Tuttle Company, 1961.

Speiser, E.A., trans. _Genesis_. Garden City: Doubleday & Company, 1964.

Sperling, Harry and Simon, Maurice, trans. _The Zohar_. London: The Soncino Press, 1978.

Watson, Burton, trans. _Chuang Tzu_. New York: Columbia University Press, 1968.

Wilmshurst, W. L. _The Meaning of Masonry_. New York: Crown, 1980.

Yampolsky, Philip B., trans. _The Platform Sutra of the Sixth Patriarch_. New York: Columbia University Press, 1967.

Zaehner, Robert C., trans. _Hindu Scriptures_. London: Dent, 1966.

135

gravity, 76, 85, 88
Great Architect, 102
Greater Mysteries, 44
Great Man, 118
Greer, R. A., 99
Gregory of Nyssa, St., xiii,
   75-77, 83, 86, 90, 94-96,
   101
Gregory Palamas, St., 114
Ground of Being, 101
Guénon, R., xiii, 17, 24-25,
   27-28, 31, 41, 49-50, 55,
   68, 79, 83, 98, 101, 104,
   109, 112, 127-128
Guide of the Perplexed, 7, 19-
   20, 28, 36, 49, 85, 93-94,
   96, 98, 114
gunas, 42-43, 101, 105, 111

Halkin, A. S., 68
Ham, 46
heart, 30, 36, 82
heaven and earth, 49, 87
Heaven and Earth, 47, 56, 59,
   66, 68, 90, 105, 108-109,
   112, 116, 121
Heaven and heavens, 2, 65, 68,
   118
heavenly food, 90
heavenly waters, 41
Heavenly Ray, 109
Hebrew people, 24
hegemony of God over the world,
   81
hell and hells, 65, 86, 118
Heraclitus, 17, 37, 109
herders and herding, 29, 31, 36
hermeneutical principle, 16
Heschel, A. J., 17
Hesse, H., 18
higher soul (mind, reason,
   intellect), 36
higher state of being, 66, 68
higher tendencies, 30-34, 54-
   55, 63-66, 75-76, 86-87,
   89, 92
Hinduism, 17, 18, 21-24, 30, 41,
   44, 49, 101-102, 109-112,
   115, 125, 128-129
Hiranygharba, 42
history, 21
Hittites, 91
Hivites, 91

Hokhmah, 102, 110
Holy of Holies, 50, 95
Holy Spirit (Ghost), 49, 109
holy war, 2, 85
Hosea, 19
House of God, 66
Hügel, F. v., 5
Hur, 91

idolatry, 23, 51
Illusion, 131
image of God, 113-118
immortality, 2, 29, 45, 125-126
imprisonment, 70-71
individuality, 1, 30, 32-33, 35,
   48, 60, 81, 126
Indra, 111
influence of Heaven, 109
initiate, 104
initiatic deaths and rebirths,
   2, 17, 50
initiatic groups, 6, 18
intellect, 30, 115
intellectual apprehension, 114-
   115
intimacy between flesh and
   spirit, 54
Iraqi, F., 108
Iris, 51
Iron Age, 21, 24, 55
Isaac, 25, 53, 57-59, 61, 63-65,
   69, 72, 85, 87
Isaiah, 125
Islam, 1
Isle of the Blessed, 123
Israel, M. b., 49
"Israel," 66, 68
Israelites, 22, 24-25, 75, 79-
   80, 85, 88-91, 94, 96-97
Isvara, 101
Izutsu, T., 108

Jacob, 25, 60, 63-68, 69-73, 85,
   87, 90
"Jacob," 68
Jacobsen, T., 27
James, 97
Jebusites, 91
Jesus, 10, 18, 39, 72, 122-123
Jethro, 76
jewelry (gold), 88-89, 97
Jews and Judaism, 1, 20, 24, 52,
   109

Seth, 25, 35
seven, 105–106
seven days of week, 106–107, 112
sex and death, 120–121
sexual awareness, 120, 125
sexual union, 28, 122–123
Shakti, 131
"shalom," 65
Shekhinah, 40, 109
Shemittot, 27
shepherd, 31, 76
Shintoism, 18, 111–112, 129
Silver Age, 21, 24
skins, 65, 77–78
sky, 42, 44, 66, 104
slavery, 23, 46–47, 55, 75, 77, 85
smiths, 29, 36
smoke, 124
Sodom, 23, 27, 53–56, 64
Solar Ray, 42, 49, 109
solidification, 31, 55
soul, 30–31, 36, 43–44, 50, 54–55, 68, 70, 82, 85, 89, 97, 122, 124
source theory of Torah, 12, 19
Speiser, E. A., 49
spider, 102
Spinoza, B., 121
spirit, 30–31, 36, 43–44, 50, 54, 70, 82, 85, 88
Spirit, 33, 35, 44, 56, 60, 112
spiritual backsliding, 70, 88
spiritual blindness, 124, 128
spiritual centers, 124
spiritual death, 51, 56, 100
spiritual influence, 25, 64–65, 104
spiritual journey (path), 56, 75–76, 85, 88, 92, 94, 96–97, 125, 127
spiritual master, 76
Spiritual Ray, 43, 57–58, 101
spiritual realization, 45–48, 60, 66, 81, 127
Spiritual (Divine) Sun, 42, 55, 75, 94, 103, 107, 109
spiritual world, 42, 50, 110, 114
spiritus, 68
sreyas, 30

stages of belief, 5–6
stairway to sky, 65–66, 68
states (realms) of being, 116–117, 124, 126
stone, 55–56
stone pillar, 66
stream of life, 39, 76
structuralistic view, 119
substance (Hyle), 41
subtle modality of human existence, 44
subtle (psychic) world (realm), 42, 49, 83, 108, 110, 114
suffering, 126–127
Sufis and Sufism, 30, 108, 118
"sulam," 65
Sumerians, 21, 27, 51
sun, 51, 81, 83
supernatural, 15
Supreme Identity, 117
Supreme Principle, 101, 104
svah, 49
swallow, 43
sweating, 104
symbolic interpretations, 8
symbols and symbolism, 8–12, 15–16, 47
Symposium, 115

tabernacle, 49, 95, 97
T'ai-chi, 102
Tai-i, 102
Tale of Two Brothers, 70
tamas, 42, 105
Tantric Buddhism and Hinduism, 128
Tao, 33, 68, 101–102, 108
Taoism, 18, 21, 28, 33, 49, 101, 124
Tao Te Ching, 33, 36, 68, 102, 108–109
tapas, 110
Te, 109
"tebah," 22
technology, 34–37, 47–48, 78
Ten Commandments, 88
ten plagues, 23, 86–88
Ten Siferot, 102, 115
Terrestrial Paradise, 56, 58, 66, 79, 115, 123–125, 127
Thales, 109
theoria, 30
three gunas, 42–43, 105, 111

144

The author received his B.A. in Philosophy from Brooklyn College and his M.A. and Ph.D. in Philosophy from the University of Michigan. His thesis was in the field of Philosophy of Religion. He began his career at Virginia Polytechnic Institute and State University and is currently Associate Professor at the University of Pittsburgh at Bradford. He is a member of both the American Philosophical Association and the American Academy of Religion. Becoming interested in Zen Buddhism while still an undergraduate he proceeded to investigate most of the spiritual traditions of the East. Realizing that many Biblical verses could be interpreted as expressing what are normally considered Eastern ideas he began systematic research into the question of whether Eastern and Western traditions really expressed the same basic truths. Adam and Eve is the first fruit of this endeavor.